The American Volunteer in Mexico

The American Volunteer in Mexico

A Civilian at War

Thomas D. Todd

WHALER BOOKS

Buena Vista, VA

Copyright © 2021 Thomas D. Todd

All rights reserved, including the right of reproduction in whole or in part in any form without the express written permission of the publisher.

1 3 5 7 9 10 8 6 4 2

Library of Congress Control Number: 2021923922

The American Volunteer in Mexico
By Thomas D. Todd
p. cm.

1. History—Military: United States
2. History—Military: Wars & Conflicts (Other)
3. History—United States: 19th Century

I. Todd, Thomas 1934– II. Title.
ISBN 13: 978-1-7378864-2-6 (softcover : alk. paper)

Design by Karen Bowen

Whaler Books
An imprint of
Mariner Media, Inc.
131 West 21st Street
Buena Vista, VA 24416
Tel: 540-264-0021
www.marinermedia.com

Printed in the United States of America
This book is printed on acid-free paper meeting the requirements of the American Standard for Permanence of Paper for Printed Library Materials.

The purpose of this book is to determine the extent, and the manners, in which the trait of undisciplined individualism affected the behavior, health, and comfort of the civilian volunteer, and as a consequence, influenced the conduct of the Mexican War by the American military authorities.

–Thomas D. Todd

Table of Contents

CHAPTER 1. THE VOLUNTEER GOES TO WAR 1

The Call to War; The Response and Maj. General Gaines; The Western Armies; Behavior and Health; Crossing the Gulf of Mexico; and, The Volunteers are Many.

CHAPTER 2. CAMP AND TOWN 15

Bad Behavior in New Mexico; Riots on the Rio Grande; Crimes and Mutiny in the Ranks; Cruelty, Kindness, and Punishment; The San Patricio Battalion and Desertion; and Panic and the Volunteers.

CHAPTER 3. HEALTH, SICKNESS, AND MISERY 31

Health in the West; Taylor's Troops in Northern Mexico; Camp Misery; Vaccination; With Scott From Vera Cruz; and Disease, Death, and Bullets.

CHAPTER 4. HEAT OF BATTLE 44

Out West with Kearney, Doniphan, and Wool; Northern Mexico and Taylor's Battles of Monterey and Buena Vista; and, the Mexican Heartland; plus

Scott's Battles of Vera Cruz, Cerro Gordo, Contreras, Churubusco, and Chapultepec.

CHAPTER 5. OPINIONS: PAST AND PRESENT.......................... 65

General Comments; Military Opinions From the Past; Opinions of Generals Taylor and Scott, President Polk, and S. Compton Smith (Surgeon in General Taylor's Army); and the Conclusion of the Author.

ENDNOTES 81

BIBLIOGRAPHY 97

Illustrations

DRAWINGS
(by Dee Todd)
Portrait of Two Volunteers x
Mouth of the Rio Grande River 10
Awaiting Execution 29
In Camp 34
Around the Fires on a Cold Night 38

MAP
(*West Point Atlas of American Wars*, Vol. 1)
The Mexican War: Summery of Operations 46

PORTRAITS
(Illustrations published in *The New Eclectic History of the United States* by M. E. Thalheimer—American Book Company; New York, Cincinnati, and Chicago—in 1881 and 1890. Copyright expired; artwork is in Public Domain. Source: Getty Images/Christine_Kohler)

Major General Zachary Taylor 72
Major General Winfield Scott 75
President James K. Polk 77

TABLE
The American Army at Buena Vista 56

Portrait of Two Volunteers by Dee Todd

Left, one of McCulloch's Texas Rangers and right, a private of Colonel Jefferson Davis' Mississippi Rifles.

Chapter 1

The Volunteer Goes to War

On the 24th of April, 1846, a patrol from General Taylor's army was ambushed by a Mexican army unit between the Nueces and the Rio Grande Rivers, resulting in sixteen killed and wounded, with the rest having no alternative but surrender.[1] News of this event prompted President Polk to submit a request for a declaration of war to Congress; which subsequently on the 13th of May responded in the affirmative. There were only sixteen negative votes in the entire Congress— two in the Senate and fourteen in the House of Representatives.[2]

While General Taylor's message was being forwarded to the capital, he was requesting of the governors of Texas and Louisiana that volunteers be sent at the earliest moment. From Texas he asked for two mounted regiments and two foot regiments; from Louisiana, four regiments of infantry. He also raised the suggestion that Congress authorize the President to call for twelve-months volunteers.[3]

Along with its declaration of war, Congress had done just that: the authority was given to the executive branch to enlist the services of a maximum of 50,000 volunteers. Immediately a call for these troops was made on the governors of the following states: Texas, Kentucky, Mississippi, Ohio, Indiana, Alabama, Georgia, Missouri, Arkansas, Illinois, and Tennessee. These troops, in twenty-six regiments—plus a battalion from the city of Baltimore and the District of Columbia—amounted to 23,000.[4] Between November of 1846 and 1847 the total number of enlisted volunteers, including the twelve-months men, was 34,853. Due, however, to various deficiencies, the net total actually sworn into service amounted to 27,452 of which 1,507 were twelve-months men. Of this number, due to losses by death, injuries and sickness, discharges and desertions, the army actually had around 20,286 combat effectives on hand.[5] These volunteers were organized into thirty regiments and six companies.[6]

General Taylor's request for Texas troops reached Governor Henderson on May 2nd in the capital at Austin. The governor immediately ordered certain counties to furnish men (and how many), with the mounted troops to report to Point Isabel and the foot soldiers to Gaveston, where mustering into the service would take place.[7] Upon receipt of General Taylor's request the state legislature of Louisiana voted $100,000 to be placed at the governor's disposal for the war. A private citizen, one Benjamin Story, Esq., gave $500,000 to the State of Louisiana upon learning of the outbreak of hostilities. Outside of the two states of Texas and Louisiana that General Taylor contacted, the first initiative was shown by a company under General Desha which departed Mobile, Alabama, on the 4th of May, en route to New Orleans. The company, one hundred strong, arrived in that city on the 5th and left for the war zone on the 6th.[8]

Maj. General Gaines, commanding the western Geographical Division—and who was the second ranking officer in the army—had been mentioned in General Taylor's request to Governor Isaac Johnson of Louisiana as a possible source of aid in organizing his volunteer troops.[9] The general, however, on his own initiative and without legal authorization, issued a call to various states for six-months volunteers. Consequently, General Taylor found himself swamped with three classes of volunteers: the three-months volunteers from Texas and Louisiana (authorized by the Act of 1795), those recruited by General Gaines, and the twelve-months volunteers raised by the national government under the Act of May 13, 1846. By the middle of June, General Taylor had more troops than he believed were needed, and even more important, more than he could provide for in the way of provisions and transportation. According to the law, the six-months volunteers could only serve for three months, or if they choose, to enlist for twelve. The majority left at the end of three months.[10] General Gaines, who had been responsible for the problem, was relieved of his command on the 10th of June and ordered to appear in Washington to face a court of inquiry.[11]

Governor Owsley of Kentucky had replied to General Gaines' letter of 15 May in the negative. He stated, that although the war effort would have the full support of the State of Kentucky, he would be in violation of his office if he acted prior to a request from the President of the United States. Shortly thereafter, on the 19th, the Governor learned from the Cincinnati and Louisville newspapers that the President was authorized to raise 50,000 volunteers, and consequently, accepted the services of one Colonel Ormsby and his eight companies who had arrived in the state capital on the 16th. He further authorized the Colonel to charter a steamboat and proceed to New Orleans without further delay.

The governor of Maryland, Thomas G. Pratt, on the 21st of May issued a call for men between 18 and 45 to volunteer for the two regiments the state had been assigned.[12] On the 27th, 260 volunteers left their camp in Howard Park, City of Baltimore, and took the train to Washington where they hoped to join with the "District Volunteers." Such a move, they believed, would hasten their arrival in the war zone. Everywhere, the enthusiasm to go to war seemed to be rampant.[13] Many, who had previously answered General Gaines' call found themselves being disbanded, having declined to change their enlistments to twelve months. The "Gunmen of West Feliciana," Louisiana,[14] Captain Desha's company (which had traveled to the war zone and back), plus six other Alabama companies and the St. Louis Legion, were all severed from the service in the midst of outraged emotions.[15]

The response to the call-to-arms within the State of Tennessee was so overwhelming, that resort to the ballot box was established as the only means of determining who would go to war.[16] The 1st Regiment, later to be known as the "Bloody First," was encamped at Camp Taylor two miles below Nashville. Here, on June 3rd, they elected their officers.[17] The 4th and 5th of June saw the men boarding the steamers, *C. Connor, Tennessee,* and *Talleyrand,* and proceeding to war; first stop, New Orleans.[18]

For the western theater of war two armies were created: the Army of the West, commanded by Brig. General Stephen Kearney (at this time a Colonel in the First Dragoons), and, the army known as the Center Division, commanded by Brig. General John E. Wool. The latter was organized at San Antonio, Texas, with its first operational goal to be the seizure of Chihuahua, Mexico; subsequently assigned, however, to Colonel Doniphan and his Mormon volunteers. The Army of the West was to be manned by volunteers from Missouri, and consequently orders were issued on the 13th and 14th of May, 1846, to this effect. General Kearney was also authorized to recruit from the Mormon immigrants who were California bound (but no more than one third of his entire army), any American settlers who volunteered, and furthermore, to requisition the State of Missouri for 1,000 mounted volunteers to follow later. When his army concentrated at Fort Bent, its strength was 1,800 men—not counting the last troops to be called—and was organized into eight companies of U.S. Dragoons, two of U.S. Artillery, two of U.S. Infantry, and nine companies of the 1st Missouri Regiment (twelve-months cavalry volunteers) under Colonel Alexander W. Doniphan.[19]

By the 9th of August seven companies of the last mounted volunteer regiment to be requested by General Kearney had gathered at Fort Leavenworth. Although three more were still expected, the others declined to wait and subsequently elected the regiment officers. Sterling Price, an ex-member of Congress, was elected Colonel; and according to the St. Louis Republican, the threat of disbandment was the power behind his election (the source of the threat not being identified). A private named Allen was elected Lieut. Colonel over the candidate favored by President Polk. On the 10th four of the companies departed en route to Santa Fe, New Mexico, with the remainder departing the following day.[20]

As the volunteers gathered at the various points in the United States—prior to departing for Mexico—tales began to circulate about their rowdiness and disregard for proper behavior. At Camp Washington, near Cincinnati, after the troops had been paid, the supply of alcohol helped to enhance the spirit of individualism as revealed by the widespread insubordination among the enlisted ranks. At Louisville there were a series of violent incidents in which knives, guns, and other weapons were utilized. A gentleman by the name of Marshall, in attempting to protect the citizenry, nearly lost his life, and a Mr. Davis was beaten so severely that his life was left hanging in doubt. One volunteer, apparently the principal culprit in the latter incident, was arrested and thrown in jail.[21]

One incident, which can only be classified as one of those unique oddities of war, occurred shortly after the Indiana volunteers were sworn into service on June 19th. The next day one of Captain Waler's company discovered that he had lost his handkerchief. Later, while at mess, he saw it protruding from the jacket of another soldier. Upon seizing it he discovered that the culprit was a young woman. She satisfied the curiosity of her fellow soldiers by stating that being without the necessary funds to join her father in Texas, she had selected the volunteers as the means of solving her problem. Passing the hat around, her new friends raised enough funds to pay for transportation to Texas of a more suitable nature for a young lady.[22]

A certain young man, J. Jacob Oswandel of Co. C, 1st Regiment Pennsylvania Volunteers, was in a theater in Pittsburgh the night before being sworn into the service. Suddenly, a mob of men from Co. D, his regiment, burst into the hall yelling, "Go in, killers! Go in, killers!" The play was temporarily halted as several altercations erupted, and then resumed when the police ejected the culprits from the building. December 18, 1846, was election day for regiment officers, and Oswandel's company sponsored their Captain William F. Small for the colonelcy. Arguing, swearing, and fist fighting were the rule as loyalties became emotionally heated. The choice of the regiment was one Francis M. Wynkoop.[23]

On the 21st they boarded steamboats, five in all, and cast off for New Orleans; arriving there on the 28th. The following morning, Capt. Small, after assuming the Officer of the Day watch, ordered the ship's captain to move the vessel to the west bank of the Mississippi River. Eight or ten soldiers, incensed that no liberty had yet been granted, went AWOL (Absent Without Leave) before the vessel could clear the wharf.[24] On January 4th, Oswandel recalls, several men were placed in the guardhouse for going into the city without permission. Worse yet, some of Co. D's men attacked a Spanish gentleman who tended a grocery and liquor store on the levee. Some of the regiment officers, who were passing by at the time, managed to save his life. The men involved (Co. D referred to themselves as the "Killers") received no punishment, and nothing was said to the colonel about it.

On January 5th, due to the lack of food and the neglect of their officers—who were generally to be found at New Orleans' St. Charles Hotel—many solders violated orders and went to town. At dress parade that afternoon about half of the men were absent, and subsequently the colonel ordered a guard detail of five men from each company to collect the AWOL's and place them in the guardhouse.[25]

A few days later, after the drill incident was over, a majority of Co. D (the Killers) went off seeking trouble. They broke into a poultry yard and carried off their loot, which included the owner's (a Frenchman) pet deer. The latter was paid for his property by the regiment officers and advised to defend his property in the future—with firearms if necessary. The following week a group of AWOL's from Co. I went to a tavern owned by a Spaniard. After taking their fill, they proceed to destroy the contents of the premises. The owner, fearing for his life and property, grabbed his gun and fired it point-blank in the face of one of the volunteers. Captain Scott of Co. H, upon receiving word of the riot, took some men and arrived in time to save the Spaniard's life. Then, the first rumor of the regiment's sailing date appeared, and four men of Co. C deserted. On embarkation day, January 16th, a dozen men from Co. D and one more from Co. C had conveniently disappeared.[27]

Also of the 1st Regiment Pennsylvania Volunteers, was one Captain Joseph Hill, who, because he felt his honor demanded first consideration, remained in New Orleans when his regiment sailed for Mexico. He recalled that Colonel Wynkoop, the regiment commander, was informed on the night of January 6, 1847, that he must restrict his men from coming into the city in large numbers. It was alleged that they were continuously breaking up dances and disturbing the peace. After it had been determined which men were missing, Captain Hill was dispatched with fifty men to arrest the AWOL's wherever they were to be found within the city. And, he was to bring them back—dead or alive! Upon reaching the city the captain acted upon information from a civilian source and headed for the location of the Washington Ball. His entry was blocked by a doorman who insisted that, "No soldiers were to be found inside." After requesting the man to step aside so he could determine the validity of the statement for himself, and being refused, Captain Hill threatened to use his men to force entry. The doorman uttered an oath and pulled out a revolver. The captain, however, drew his sword a faction faster, and with his men shoved the doorman aside and entered the vestibule. There they were met by the proprietor. After a brief discussion the captain was allowed to enter the ballroom, his men remaining behind. After seizing six regiment men trying to depart by way of a window, the captain found himself being informed that he was under arrest. The author of that action, by the name of Whitmore, was then seized by the captain's men, who in their turn, discovered their path out blocked by the city police. The matter was finally resolved by the acceptance of Captain Hill's word that he considered himself their prisoner and would return when requested; a compromise initiated by the officials' belief that the soldiers' guns were loaded. They weren't!

The next day the captain extended his apologies as a means of pacifying the city officials, and believed the matter to be settled. On the 16th, however, as the regiment was boarding ship to depart New Orleans, he found himself under arrest by the ballroom proprietor and two police officers for alleged damages. When he insisted that he could not go with them at that time, they accepted his word that he would meet them at 4 that afternoon. After Colonel Wynkoop had refused to place his order of January 6th in writing—thereby relieving the captain of responsibility—and had ordered Hill to remain on board, the captain submitted his resignation (to become effective in Washington in 30 days) and left the ship. Captain Hill later rejoined his command in Mexico.[28]

While in New Orleans the troops of the "Bloody First," for the most part, were restricted to their quarters in order to expedite any sudden departure for Mexico. Those who did get to enjoy the delights of the city, observed the proprieties sufficiently well to render praise by the local newspapers. After successive days and nights of warding off blood-hungry mosquitos in confining quarters, the men were glad to depart on the evening of the 17th of January.[29]

While Captain Desha's company was on the Rio Grande, two of his men, both sergeants, deserted and were later arrested in Mobile, Alabama. Hauled before a civil court, the judge ruled that only a military court had jurisdiction and the men were subsequently turned over to the nearest military authorities. From the ranks of the Georgia volunteers, two men—Farrar and McNier—drowned in the Alabama River while en route to Mobile. They were attempting to desert and return home. Later, while in Mobile, some members of this same regiment were harassing some blacks at the wharf. Two were thrown or knocked into the water, with the resulting death of one lad. Of the three volunteers arrested, two were later released while the third was sentenced to a term in prison.[30] Another volunteer, one Henry Grammont, was brought before Judge McCaley, U.S. District Court, New Orleans, charged with deserting from Fort Jackson, Louisiana. The judge ruled in Grammont's favor and set him free. The reasons were: Grammont had been enlisted under the call issued by General Gaines which had no legal basis, and furthermore, said defendant had offered his service to aid General Taylor in Mexico—not to man a stateside garrison.[31]

The 1st Pennsylvania Regiment, while waiting in Pittsburgh to embark for New Orleans, had been quartered in a large warehouse with no heat or facilities for alleviating their distress. Because of the cold weather many of the men sought more adequate quarters in the city at their own expense. Oswandel and others like him, more used to hardships in life, laughed at these city fellows and stated that they had better get used to it.[32] No one was prepared, however, when the regiment departed New Orleans and entered the Gulf of Mexico. Having partaken of a dinner of fat pork and bean soup shortly before, the rolling and pitching of the ship caused the stomachs of all to turn inside out. The ship was one mass scene of men laying about, holding their stomachs and groaning, or heaving over the rails.[33]

The members of the "Bloody First" had some similar experiences during their voyage to Mexico. After being packed aboard a rather small ship, they discovered that there was insufficient room for all 500 men, including the crew, to lie down. As soon as they passed the mouth of the Mississippi River seasickness set in, and the scene was one of a crowded, suffocating stench. Those above couldn't go below, while those below were unable to make their way to the open decks, and all were forced to stand or lay in their own filth. To heighten their discomfort the water had become intolerable due to improper casks having been utilized.[34]

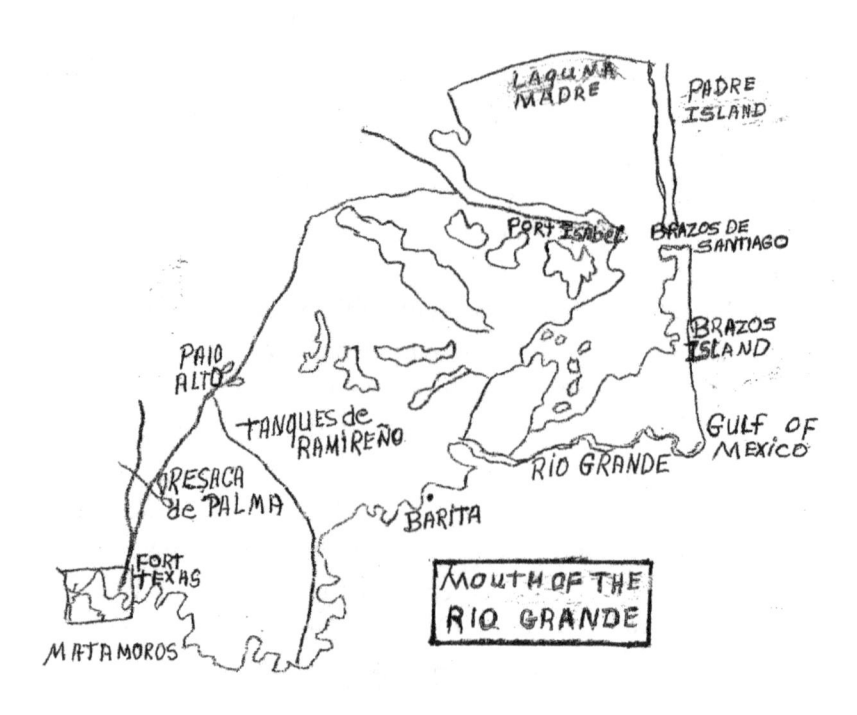

S. Compton Smith, who later became General Taylor's Acting Surgeon, had joined the 1st Regiment of Texas Rifles which sailed to the war zone aboard the schooner *Rosella*. The less-than-seaworthy vessel was packed with only three days ration, instead of seven; and, the men feared for their lives. Two days out a storm struck, and everything which was not lashed down was swept overboard, Finally the sails and masts were all torn and swept away, and water entered through opened seams. Being near shore the ship's captain drove onto the beach, each man trusting to his own strength and luck to reach safety. Their haven was Padre Island, extending between Corpus Christi and Brazos de Santiago. Since the southern end of the island was opposite Brazos Island, and thus near Point Isabel, rescue was soon effected.[35]

> Upon our arrival at Point Isabel, we proceeded with the business of electing our regimental officers. Selected as our regimental colonel was one General A. Sidney Johnson. After a few weeks we were ordered to march to Comargo, but, because General Taylor wanted only twelve months men and our enlistment was for six, we were paid off and mustered out of the service. The majority of the men joined other units which were under regulation.[36]

Those aboard the ship *Ondieka* also had the experience of being shipwrecked. Four companies of the Louisiana Regiment of Volunteers sailed from Balize on the 20th of January, 1847. On the 28th the ship was reported off Tampico, and then came news of the ship's disaster—apparently near the Island of Lobos. Colonel De Russy, after he and his men had struggled ashore, was hailed by General Cos of the Mexican Army to surrender to his force of 1,800 strong; although in truth he only had 980 men. The Americans were given until 9 a.m. the following day to determine their answer. Shortly after night had fallen the colonel ordered campfires to be kindled, the men to discard everything that they could do without, and then led the troops on the beginning of a long walk to escape the enemy's trap. They were undetected, and in the first twenty-four hours covered thirty-five miles. Exhausted, they straggled into Tampico—which was occupied by American forces—on the 4th of February.[37]

In the northern theater, in Santa Fe, New Mexico, General Kearney commanded 2,700 troops, the majority being volunteers from Missouri.[38] Prior to his departure for California, Kearney ordered Colonel Doniphan to lead his 1st Missouri Volunteers to Chihuahua, Mexico, to aid General Wool;[39] and Colonel Price, to remain in command of the occupation forces of New Mexico.[40] In addition to these troops in Santa Fe, General Kearney had 1,300 other troops throughout New Mexico. Of his total force of 4,000 combatants, only 446 were regular army. To the south-east General Wool's Central Division consisted of 2,660 combatants; 621 regular, and 2,039 volunteers.[41]

At Camargo, Mexico, by October 1846, General Taylor's army consisted of Butler's, Worth's, and Twigg's Divisions for a total of 6,640 troops. Butler's Division, referred to as the "Volunteer Division," consisted of Hamer's Brigade (1,080 men)—Colonel Mitchell's 1st Regiment Ohio Volunteers (540 men) and Colonel Armsby's 1st Regiment Kentucky Volunteers (540 troops)—and Quitman's Brigade (1,630 men) for a total of 2,710 troops; plus Colonel's Campbell's 1st Regiment Tennessee Volunteers (540 troops), Colonel Jefferson Davis's 1st Regiment Mississippi Rifles (690 men), and Colonel Watson's Baltimore Battalion (400 men). Within General North's Division, Colonel P. Smith's regiment (500 men), and the two Texas Ranger companies (120 men) of McCullough's and Gillespie's were the only volunteers out of 1,700 troops. Out of Twigg's Division of 2,230 men, only Colonel Hays' 500 Texas horsemen were volunteers. Between Carmargo and Brazos, under Maj. General Patterson and Brig. Generals Marshall, Pillow, Lane, and Shields, were 9,170 more troops—

thus giving General Taylor a total force of 15,810.[42] By January 2, 1847, the total army strength engaged in the war amounted to nearly 25,000 combat troops.[43]

Chapter 2

Camp and Town

The lack of propriety which the volunteers often manifested in their off-the-battlefield behavior, was just as likely to be directed at one another as it was toward unarmed Mexican civilians. Susan Magoffin, the wife of a trader, travelled with Colonel Doniphan and his Missourians from Santa Fe to Mexico, and soon learned that peace and quiet were not the cherished values of that group of volunteers. A continuous roar hung over the various camp sites for the largest portion of each stop; included in which, were expressions of a shocking nature to her feminine ears.

George Ruxton, an Englishman, described the camp scene at Valverde on the Rio Grande in the following manner. The tents were in a straight line, but any other evidence of order or cleanliness was not to be found: garbage littered the ground, personal cleanliness was entirely a forgotten habit—if it had ever been one—and dress showed only a loose sense of conformity. The men spent their camp time gambling, fighting, and swearing; and woe to the officer who was foolish enough to try and instill discipline into such a chaotic mess. And because they decided—

the rank and file that is—that sentries were unnecessary (what is more likely, the idea didn't appeal to them), approximately eight hundred sheep were stolen by Navajo Indians, while their horses and mules wandered wherever the next blade of grass beckoned.[1] Later, however, these same men (there were slightly over 900) would defeat a Mexican force of four times their number at Sacramento Pass, Mexico.[2]

Behind them in northern New Mexico, trouble was simmering just under the surface; agitated in large part by the undisciplined behavior of the 1,700 volunteers who had remained as occupation troops. Lieut. Jeremy Gilmer of the regular army was disturbed by the lack of propriety exhibited by the volunteers when interacting with the local citizens. Boastful braggarts, they acted without regard for anyone else, praising the United States while degrading everything Mexican or Spanish. To counter the increasing tension the guard system was improved, and a curfew was enforced after ten in the evening.[3] Colonel Price, the commanding officer, was able to crush an uprising in the Taos area, but other than the action noted above, he made no attempt to control the behavior of the volunteer. Either he didn't want to (because he was elected to his colonelcy), or he was incompetent to do so. Officers were observed dealing Monte in the gambling dens of Santa Fe, and enlisted men betting on the cards which were dealt. A reporter for an eastern newspaper, the *St. Louis Missouri Republican*, made this observation:

> We arrived in Santa Fe on the 25th of June—we see the most miserable state of society that exists upon the wide globe. Lewdness in both sexes exhibits itself in the most glaring and shameless forms, and walks abroad at midday, as if the human family had dwindled down to nothing more than brute intellect and less than savage refinement. True, there are many of the officers and privates of Colonel Price's regiment who are

gentlemen—However, the vast majority have expended more than the amount of their wages and are, indeed, a reckless ragamuffin band, a disgrace to the name of American soldiers.[4]

One volunteer, writing home in December of 1846, stated that Colonel Price was so incompetent that Washington wouldn't be able to save him from General Kearny's wrath—if the latter should return. Although the writer expressed no personal animosity toward Colonel Price, he stated that the man's unfair obtainment of his rank called for retribution of some kind—from some quarter.[5] The following spring, the *Daily National Intelligencer* of Washington, D.C., reported that the Taos insurrection would not have occurred had a more competent officer been in charge of the occupational forces. The regulars, the newspaper claimed, were respected and popular with the Mexicans, while the majority of the volunteers are the most lawless of men; and their officers, allegedly, are not fit to be corporals in the regular army. The volunteer system, the Washington paper insisted, was at most a bad bulwark for the country in time of war.[6]

Proceeding to the banks of the Rio Grande River and General Taylor's army, we will examine some incidences which illustrate how the volunteer's wrath could erupt just as violently upon his fellow soldiers as on the Mexican civilians. First of all, there was an incident which took place at Camp Belknap near Burita around the end of July, first of August, 1846. The Baltimore Battalion with the 1st Ohio Battalion formed a regiment, and with two other Ohio regiments, constituted a Brigade. Andrew Metteer and some friends, all of the Baltimore Battalion, were returning to camp from Burita when someone gave him a recently caught catfish. They were entering camp when Colonel Mitchell of the 1st Ohio, who was also the regimental commander, stepped forward and claimed the fish. When the colonel ordered three men to seize the fish, Metter flashed his knife and cut two of them, whereupon Colonel Mitchell inflicted several gashes on Metter's head dropping him to the riverbank.

Lafayette Hands, a friend of Metter's, tore the sword from the colonel's hand and proceeded to chase the defenseless officer. Someone handed the colonel another sword, and the chase became a swordfight; that is, until the latter's sword broke. Escaping to his quarters Colonel Mitchell yelled orders for the 2,500 Ohioians to turn out with arms.[7] As the Ohioians ran down to the river, the cry, "Turn out Baltimoreans!" echoed through the camp.[8] The latter—600 strong—grabbed their weapons and headed for the river.[9] Captain John Kenly of the Baltimore Battalion, joined by Lieut. Colonel Weller of the 1st Ohio and other officers, over the course of several tense minutes, managed to persuade the men to disperse and return to their duties.[10]

An even more violent encounter between volunteer units occurred at Camp Belknap while boarding river boats for Camargo. The Georgia regiment was divided between boats, with Lieut. Colonel Redd and four companies of the regiment boarding the third steamer. Two of these companies, plus an Illinois regiment, became involved in a riot. The four Georgia companies were identified as follows: the Jasper Greens, Captain McMahon; the Kenesaw Rangers, Captain Nelson; the Fanning Avengers, Captain Sargent; and the Canton Volunteers, Captain Byrd. The two companies in question, the Greens and the Rangers, had been assigned locations on the upper deck. As the two companies filed on board the Greens went to the right and the Rangers to the left, both finding themselves at the bottom of a gangplank which led from the center below to the left and right of the deck above. Suddenly the Greens, who were armed to the teeth, were observed using their weapons on the "unarmed Rangers." The disturbance was quickly smothered by Lieut. Colonel Redd and others. Captains McMahon and Nelson, who had come down from the upper deck to help, had ordered the sentries to allow none of the troops on the upper deck to come below. They were soon overpowered, however, and the battle raged anew. Finally the officers gained control—Captain Nelson ordering his men ashore, and Captain McMahon directing his to the upper deck. The few Rangers who had remained there found themselves being defended by Captain McMahon, whose men were not inclined to let the matter drop. At this point Colonel Baker and twenty-five men of his Illinois Volunteers were returning from a burial detail. He offered his services to Lieut. Colonel Redd, and upon their acceptance, rushed to the upper deck of the steamer with his men. Finding the Captain earnestly attempting to gain control of his men, he called on the Greens to surrender. The captain spun around, sword in hand and rage on his face, "Damn you, measure swords with me!" As they fought a pistol shot rang out, killing the colonel. As the officer fell to the deck, the next senior officer ordered his men to run the captain through. They did! The Greens then assaulted the Illinois men—of whom half ended up in physically damaged condition. With the shot that killed the colonel, Corporal Whalen of the Greens, who was using his bayonet to prevent Rangers from gaining the upper deck, fell dead from a ball through the heart. In all, four men, two enlisted and two officers, were killed in this riot.[11]

Colonel Jack Hays' regiment of Texas Rangers, having participated in the capture of Monterey, had entered the city of September 21, 1846. One of the rangers, Harrison Beal, had served out his enlistment and stayed on in the city as owner of a saloon and restaurant. One Sunday morning while riding across the plaza at a fast clip, he encountered the colonel of the Massachusetts Regiment proceeding in the other direction. The colonel, who was occasionally a customer at Beal's establishment, reacted to the greeting, "Good morning, Colonel," with a question of, "Why in hell he rode so fast?" Beal slowed momentarily and replied that he was in a hurry to meet some friends. The colonel shouted at the nearby guardhouse—manned by a Massachusetts Volunteer—"Shoot down that damned Texan!" And the soldier shot Beal dead. The body was left for several hours in a corner of the guardhouse, and then thrown into a pit, Beal's friends removed the body and subsequently gave him a decent burial.

A few days later the Massachusetts Regiment was ordered to proceed to Matamoros and then on to Vera Cruz to join General Scott. As the troops crossed the Virgin's Bridge, one Irish trooper, drunk, refused to budge another inch. After some initial confusion the order rang out, "Shoot the damned rascal!" A nearby comrade—also drunk—placed the muzzle of his weapon to the head of the obstinate solder and did exactly that. And then the regiment moved on, leaving the dead soldier lying on the bridge.[12]

The "Bloody First" Regiment had their first court martial at Lomita; the case was larceny, and the accused was convicted of the crime. The day following the end of the trial, the prisoner was drummed out of the service in full view of his fellow soldiers. He was forced to mount a long pole with rope and rawhide stirrups of different lengths, which was then hoisted to the shoulders of several men who moved off through the troops. The prisoner found himself performing acrobatic feats of an amazing nature, which were quite unintentional, and amidst the volume of jeers and cheers which filled the air.[13]

J. Jacob Oswandel, of the 1st Pennsylvania Regiment, maintained a diary while in Mexico and provides us with several interesting incidents. One morning the Sergeant Major ordered a detail of five men per company to report to Colonel Wynkoop for a work detail which involved sweeping. The men told the colonel that they had not joined the army to be slaves, and if necessary, would hire sweepers out of their own pockets. They had their way.[14]

On another occasion he wrote in his diary that several New York Volunteers had been confined to the guardhouse for breaking into and looting a ranch house, and also, for disorderly conduct within camp. These New Yorkers, he stated, were nearly all of a brutal nature, fighting anyone and everyone like the things they were.[15]

Trouble meant courts martial, and Oswandel noted that two privates of the 2nd Maryland Regiment were convicted of sleeping on watch and sentenced to face a firing squad. One volunteer, one James B. Wilson, while under the influence of alcohol, stole a pair of socks. For this crime he was sentenced to imprisonment in the castle of San Juan de Ulloa, to be confined in irons at hard labor, to forfeit his pay, have his head shaved, and then at the war's end, to be dishonorably discharged from the army.[16] Another volunteer, Thomas Karr of Co. G, 1st Regiment Pennsylvania Volunteers, also received an equally severe sentence—to be confined within the walls of the Castle of Chapultepec—for striking a non-commissioned officer. Still another court martial tried a horse stealing case involving members of both the New York and South Carolina regiments. These individuals were on guard duty at the time General Cushing's horse was spirited away, and apparently evidence indicated that the defendants were the culprits.[17]

In addition to the aforementioned offenses, plus the other examples of misconduct, there has to be added that of mutiny. The first example was the one called "Paine's Mutiny." After Buena Vista, the war in northern Mexico declined into occasional encounters with guerrilla forces, and time became increasingly heavy for the undisciplined volunteers. To counteract the effects of increased boredom, many commanding officers attempted to impose tighter discipline, ignoring the causes. Such attempts by elected officers with little or no military experience, resulted in failure in many forms. In the case of Colonel Paine and the Virginia, Mississippi, and North Carolina regiments, it was the form just mentioned—mutiny. Although General Wool and a court-of-inquiry upheld Colonel Paine and imposed punishment on the offenders, the President saw it otherwise—at least in one respect. Although he upheld the colonel in approving the sentences of a majority of the offenders, he did restore the commissions, and issued pardons, to the two officers who had failed to aide the colonel during the mutiny. Votes were considered too important to allow justice to interfere![18]

Another incident which bordered on mutiny, concerned a member of Captain Mear's company of mounted volunteers. The culprit had threatened and then attempted to take his captain's life. While under the sentence of death, Captain Mearwrote a letter to the court martial board requesting a reduction of the sentence. The request was denied! The execution was conducted in view of the entire company. The first volley failed to kill the prisoner, and after his request for water was fulfilled, his suffering was ended.[19]

Dr. S. Compton Smith, of the 1st Texas Rifles, related an incident between the volunteers of his regiment and the commissary officer. The latter, a "West Pointer," was extremely prejudiced against all volunteers and let no opportunity pass that would allow him to express it. The lieutenant had purchased an amount of corn which was stored in a building where a number of handmills were also located, and some of the troops requested some of the corn, and also, the loan of a handmill for grinding. They were refused! That is, loan of a handmill was refused. The corn they could have. The handmills were intended, the lieutenant claimed, for the regular troops at Monterey. Appealing to Dr. Smith, who outranked the lieutenant, they were advised to take the mills they needed, replacing them when the corn had been ground. Later that day the doctor called upon the young officer who was in a towering rage. Those "blackguard volunteers," as he contemptuously referred to them, had taken every mill they could find and were grinding, singing, and worst of all—were ignoring him! The lesson had its effect however, for thereafter the lieutenant was more open to reason.[20]

One evening while in camp, John G. Craig of Co. C, 1st Regiment Pennsylvania Volunteers, went on guard duty in the middle of the night. Around 2 o'clock in the morning he heard something moving toward him and called, "Who comes there?" There was no answer. Only silence. In panic he fired—and hearing something fall, relaxed. When daylight broke he cautiously approached the spot and saw to his amazement and chagrin that his victim was a jackass. Thereafter he was required to suffer the taunts of his comrades as they would cry out: "Who shot the jackass? John G. Craig of Co. C."[21]

Following the occupation of Monterey in September of 1846, American volunteers were being trapped in out-of-the-way spots and coldly murdered. In a report dated December 1, 1846, a correspondent for the *New Orleans Delta* related that some forty Mexicans had been murdered in retaliation, fifteen in one day within a one-square-mile area. The Louisville Legion of Kentucky had taken on the role of executioner.[22] During the same period there was also extensive looting and rape, plus burning of thatched huts belonging to local peasants. And these outrages were only the beginning: over one hundred Mexicans were killed within a couple of months, including a Mexican soldier who had a pass from General Worth. He was shot down in broad daylight in the main street by a Texas volunteer. According to the *Charleston Mercury*:

> The volunteers and their barbaric behavior have had a direct and definite bearing on the successful termination of the war. The Mexicans themselves admit that prior to the arrival of the volunteers upon the Rio Grande, all Eastern Mexico was ripe for revolt and annexation to the United States. Now there is no portion of the country so hostile to us.[23]

In February of 1847 a member of the Arkansas cavalry was murdered by Mexicans. Retaliation was quick and brutal: descending on the village of Catana the volunteers killed and wounded without concern for sex or age.[24] Such had also been the fate of the little village of Burita. Because the volunteers had so little to do while in camp, they made it a habit to roam the countryside. Consequently the local people became afraid of them and fled whenever they approached. A regular army officer, who passed through during the summer of 1846, noticed many of the Louisiana volunteers fighting and drinking in the town from which the inhabitants had fled.[25]

During the morning of May 3, 1847, Jacob Oswandel and company were preparing to continue their march toward Mexico City; thankful to be leaving their miserable camp. Around 12 noon the Cameron Guards of Harrisburg, Pennsylvania, 2nd Regiment Pennsylvania Volunteers, halted in front of Colonel Wm. B. Roberts's tent and requested food. When they received a negative reply they descended in mob form on the Mexican huckster women, who sold food items within the camps, and took all they possessed. All attempts to stop them were useless as they plundered and then drove the women from camp. The eatables were then passed around.

The following day a Catholic priest was robbed of a gold cross and watch attached to a gold chain. John (Pat) O'Brien of Co. D (the Killers), 1st Regiment Pennsylvania Volunteers, was arrested and charged with the crime. His defense was assigned to Lieut. Colonel Black and Captain Small. That the trial resulted in an acquittal was not surprising; inasmuch as Pat's friends swore that he was ill at the time, and, of course with Captain Small's interest in justice motivated by his fee of one stolen gold watch.[26]

On the 16th of June, 1847, General Taylor reported that the twelve-months volunteers, traveling to the Gulf of Mexico on their way home, had committed just about every known offense on the helpless natives along the way.[27] Of all the volunteers, the Texans, and especially the "Texas Rangers," demonstrated the utmost cruelty toward the Mexican people, civilians and unarmed soldiers alike. Ranging abroad day and night in search of guerrillas, they killed all they encountered. Prisoners were never taken![28] As the general stated, they have "scarcely made one expedition without unwarrantably killing a Mexican."[29] On one occasion they raided the hacienda of San Juan de Estancia, the property of guerrilla chief, Colonel Don Mariano Cenobio, and upon finding him absent, fired all of the buildings without exception.[30] These rangers were especially repulsive to General Taylor's sense of moral decency; and subsequently, he ordered them to Saltillo where they would have less opportunity to kill indiscriminately. Furthermore, he requested that no more troops be sent to his command from the State of Texas.[31]

The tendencies illustrated by the New Yorkers resulted in as many acts of barbarism in Scott's army as the Texans had committed while attached to Taylor's. One example is that of Nicholas Dorich, who had been hired by one Colonel Kinney to procure supplies for the American troops. When General Patterson's Division of Volunteers passed Dorich's residence, "all hell broke loose!" The troops forced their way through his front door with an axe, and although he proved his Spanish nationality, they continued to harass him. A captain seeking to protect Dorich was knocked down, and the latter attacked with many resulting wounds. When the captain advised Dorich that he couldn't protect him, the latter fled to the woods with the New York volunteers in hot pursuit. They overtook him, stripped him of his clothes, and left him for whatever fate would decide. One soldier, in attempting to protect him, was wounded by a bayonet. The volunteers destroyed his well, and stole $500 in American gold which was legally his property. Later that evening, some other American soldiers found him and gave him some clothes.[32]

During the Battle of Cerro Gordo the opposite of their cruel behavior was demonstrated. Dr. Pedro Linden, Surgeon General of the Mexican Army, was operating at a field hospital when an attack made the Mexican cavalry retreat toward Corral Falso. The doctor and his staff continued the operation—an amputation—without regard to their own safety, although the shells were passing close by and the shouts of the Americans were coming nearer. Immediately after the completion of the operation a number of volunteers appeared, and seeing the Mexican uniforms yelled, "Death to the Mexican officers." Placing himself in front of their guns, Dr. Linden held up his bloody hands which still gripped part of the mutilated leg of his last patient and cried, "Respect humanity or a hospital of blood—we are surgeons." At that moment, an officer named Pion stepped in between and raised the volunteer's guns with his sword. The Americans turned and commenced bringing in the wounded without regard to their nationality or army. The Mexican doctors in turn, were not found lacking in the same spirit, as they operated and treated only according to the principles of humanity. The volunteers denied them nothing that would aid them and the wounded.[33]

Following the battle just mentioned, some members of the "Bloody First" were on the battlefield when an Indian mother, widowed, was observed looking among the bodies for her only child. Having come twenty miles in her search, she at last found him, tied the body to a chair and strapped the burden to her back. As she passed the volunteers who watched, her sad countenance caused them to speak words of sympathy. The words which poured from her throat were little understood, but the grief in voice and gestures conveyed her message of sorrow and anguish.[34]

Late in November of 1847 a court martial passed the sentence of death upon two American teamsters who had been convicted of killing a Mexican boy. Most of the troops in and around Jalapa were ordered out for guard duty at the hanging the following day. Oswandel's regiment was stationed around the gallows, and he thus observed the approach of the two prisoners, the actual event, and long remembered, that one died struggling.[35] Another execution took place in Saltillo in early January of 1848. The prisoner, Alexander Neuson, of Captain Mear's company, had murdered a Mexican in Calle Real. At about 10:30 a.m. a wagon pulled by four horses and escorted by guards halted under the gallows. The prisoner, clothed in white and extremely drunk, rose from beside the coffin which was to be his final resting place. Captain Duggan, North Carolina Volunteers, the Officer of the Day, approached the condemned man and placed the noose around his neck. While two soldiers held the man up—he was too intoxicated to stand alone—he denied his name and stated that only two men in the brigade knew what his real name was. Then he died.[36]

The American army was also plagued with the curse of desertion. The 7th Regiment alone lost around 120 men in this manner between September 25, 1846, and the end of the year. The regulars usually deserted to the enemy; the volunteers, however, usually went no further than the nearest European settlement.[37] While the regulars were inclined to believe the worst of the volunteers, in the matter of desertions, it was they who possessed the greatest disgrace. Only one glaring example is needed to substantiate that claim: the "San Patricio Battalion!" This battalion of the Mexican Army was manned by deserters from the regular forces of the United States. These individuals deserted to the enemy for religious reasons, or simply, because they didn't know where else to go. General Arista, of the Mexican Army, had issued a proclamation in April, 1846, inviting American soldiers to desert to the Mexican side.[38] From the *El Reublicano of Mexico*, the following information was obtained:

> We had the pleasure on Sunday last of seeing a company of American deserters, principally Irish, reviewed by his excellency the general in chief. They are

perfectly armed and equipped, and are on the point of departure for Tula. This company have made a peculiar standard for themselves, on one side of which is seen the national coat of arms, with the motto, "Long live the republic of Mexico." On the other side is a figure of St. Patrick, their patron.[39]

A great many Irish and German immigrants were to be found in the regular forces of the United States; and those who were of the Roman Catholic faith saw a common bond between themselves and the Mexican people. The invitation of the Mexicans to desert, which included free land, was directed toward such emotional ties. The volunteers cannot escape part of the responsibility—at least for those who deserted after the commencement of the war—for certainly tales of their mistreatment of the Mexican people reached the ears of these new Americans from the Old World. These deserters fought with the desperation of those who feared capture more than death; to the point, that they killed Mexican comrades who were trying to surrender at Churubusco. Some, however, were captured.

On the 9th of September, 1847, sixteen deserters were hung and ten or twelve whipped at San Angel. The latter were also branded on the cheek with the capital letter "D." Major Riley, the leader of the San Patricio Battalion, because he had deserted prior to the declaration of war, consequently escaped the hangman and instead suffered the whip and the branding iron. General Twiggs had a Mexican musketeer flog the Major in place of an American soldier; considering such to be a fitting disgrace for such a man. The following day four more were hung at Miscone, and then on the 13th, thirty were hanged en masse upon the same gallows after watching the Americans storm Chapultepec. Colonel Harney, in charge of the execution, made it a point to ensure that their last sight would be the American flag rising above the city. It was![41] The following spring, Maj. General Bulter, successor to General Scott in Mexico, pardoned the remainder of those who had belonged to the San Patricio Battalion.[42]

The largest case of desertion among the volunteers occurred in the Louisiana Mounted Regiment commanded by Captain White. During March 1848, 2nd Lieutenant John Smith deserted with seven of his men. The captain upon hearing of the desertion, gave pursuit on the Orizaba Road, but was unable to catch the fugitives. That night, a young soldier of about 19 years—one of the deserters—returned to camp. He claimed that he had been mislead—that he had been told that the party was going hunting. About eight miles from camp the lieutenant had announced their intention of becoming bandits. Refusing to enlist in the scheme the young man at first feared for his

Awaiting Execution

U.S. deserters who had joined the Mexicans watch the fighting near Chapultepec, their necks in nooses. They were hanged at the moment of American victory.

life, but finally they let him go. The following day the deserters encountered Aenobia (or Cenobio), a Mexican guerrilla and bandit. Not trusting the hated Americans, and believing it to be a fine trick on his unwanted guests, he sent word to Governor Wilson in Vera Cruz. One Captain Kerr was detailed with a patrol to arrest the deserters and escort them to the aforementioned city. Lieutenant Smith, prior to deserting, had been under arrest in his quarters for misappropriation of government funds; thus, accounting in part for his desire to seek a new life in Mexico.[43]

Volunteers were offered bounties for enlisting, and knowing that there would be many who would seek to swindle their country, the government posted rewards for the arrest of such individuals. By the first part of 1847 the rewards which had been paid out amounted to over $33,300. Such was the price for the arrest of 1,011 deserters from the Army of the United States.[44]

Chapter 3

Health, Sickness, and Misery

Although the volunteers proved in large part that they were a hardy lot; disease and exposure took a grim toll far exceeding the number of deaths on the battlefield.[1] As General Winfield Scott so aptly stated the case, part of the problem was to be found in their general lack of discipline. "The volunteers," he said, "often eat their supper cold, fail to erect their tents, and sleep exposed to the elements; subsequently ending up in an early grave or the hospital."[2]

On August 24, 1846, an Illinois volunteer in Texas wrote that the troops were in fairly good physical condition; although a mild form of measles had spread among the companies. There was a sick station at Camp Irwin and another at Sevilla Creek; the latter under the care of Dr. Hope, and commanded by one Captain Webb. The total number left behind at the time amounted to approximately 200 men, one third of whom were sick with the rest filling the role of nurses.[3]

Another volunteer, with Colonel Price in Santa Fe, New Mexico, wrote on the 19th of November, 1846, to the *Columbia Statesman* concerning the general well-being of the troops there. A state of sickness was to be found throughout the army's ranks, he reported, the great majority of them being volunteers. As many as seven deaths a day had been reported—and their mounts were to fare no better if forage continued to be unavailable. The fact that they had not received any pay hampered them in buying their own supplies, and thus greatly added to their discontent.[4] The winter of 1846–47, which swept down on New Mexico with unusual fierceness, confined the troops to their quarters for the majority of the days. Time lagged and boredom became common. The state of health however had improved over that of the fall, and in the opinion of Dr. DeCamp it was tolerable, considering the circumstances. He wrote:

> The number of troops which have come to Santa Fe, since the 18th day of August last, is 4,800, and the deaths which have occurred among them since that time, amount to 120. To persons unaccustomed to see large bodies of men brought suddenly together as an army, this might seem a great mortality, but when the calculation is made and the percentage proved to be on 2%, on the whole number, it will be found that it is not greater, if as great, as takes place with the same number of persons in civil life in the upper counties of Missouri.

Death had found its victims, in view of the doctor's statement, mainly among the country troops. The St. Louis companies—three in total—enjoyed good health because of their alleged better discipline and cleanliness. Further, the doctor believed that the corrupt and vicious native population of Santa Fe deserved a large share of the blame for the excesses the troops committed in their daily activities. When a large body of men are placed without restraints in such a situation, better behavior can hardly be expected; and consequently, the general health is always threatened.[5]

Quite a number of volunteers—and it will be remembered that they were from Missouri—were suffering from various ailments at the time of their entry into New Mexico. Many of these ailments and diseases had their origin in one of the three overflows of Missouri River which had occurred in the years just prior to the war. Others, who had suffered from one complaint or another for years, came in the hope that the climate would improve their health. Another factor, was the preparation of food by the volunteers themselves; where before they had relied on those skilled in the task. As proof of his statements, Dr. DeCamp declared, that not one dragoon (regulars who had mounts, but dismounted to fight) had experienced death since arriving in New Mexico.[6] Furthermore, before the winter had exhausted its power, a fever—of a typhoid nature—struck the area and rendered all but 300 volunteers unfit for duty.[7]

In the days following the arrival of the "Bloody First" in Mexico, the men who suffered most from the sea voyage began to recover their strength. The food, plentiful and good, included crabs, fish, and occasionally some sheep or goat meat. Such fare, plus the exercise of sea bathing, swiftly erased the marks of their recent journey.[8] At Lomita their camp was on a good location with only one flaw—their nearest wood supply was three miles away. This difficulty was overcome by hiring several Mexican peasants with carts and oxen. The heat of the day was dissipated after ten in the morning by the light sea breeze which made its appearance for the remainder of the day.

Soon, however, the camp's sick population shot upward as swarms of flies suddenly appeared, making eating in particular a tricky business. Mosquitoes, nicknamed the "night fowls," relieved the flies as darkness fell and continued the harassing tactics throughout the night. Next, measles made an appearance, and due to the wet ground which served as a bed, many cases led to an early and unexpected grave. With the rainy season the wet ground soon became a quagmire.[9] On the 25th of August, 1847, the "Bloody First" established a new camp on the San Juan River, four miles above its junction with the Rio Grande River. The site had to be cleared of the cactus phyllanthus (which were five to ten feet tall), a chore which required a week for the several regiments to complete. Since the camp was surrounded by low, rocky hills on three sides, and the San Juan River on the other; the troops were cut off from the sea breeze while being subjected to the prostrating heat of the sun's rays as they were reflected off the hills. Many men were struck down by this oven-like heat, while others were attacked by an endemic diarrhea from drinking the brackish water of the river. And to heap misery upon more misery, measles were still in residence.[10]

S. Compton Smith revealed that the general health of the troops improved with their movement away from the coast

In Camp

and into the higher elevations. The main beneficiaries were the sufferers from dysentery and diarrhea. Although deaths were still reported, they were caused by diseases which the individuals had when they arrived and not by those that were contracted afterwards.[11]

A letter from Colonel Samuel R. Curtis, Commanding Officer of the 3rd Regiment Ohio Volunteers, September 7, 1846, gave a picture of improvement among his troops in Mexico. Although he reported 150 men sick, this was a smaller percentage of his regiment than when they had been at Camp Washington. Commenting that very few battles have ever cost an army more than five percent of its manpower, he added that disease alone had decimated his regiment from its original strength of 780 to 620 men. Some regiments suffered even more, and not all by death. Hundreds passed down the banks of the Rio Grande River, heading home with medical certificates attesting to their incurable conditions. Many a grave along the banks of the Rio Grande and the Gulf of Mexico became a witness to one who didn't complete the homeward journey.[12]

During the day of August 29, 1846, a requisition was received for five hundred troops of the "Bloody First" to proceed to Monterey. When the regiment was formed on parade for the selection of those to go, it was discovered, due to the effect of death and disease, that there weren't enough men to honor the request. Disease had destroyed the health, lives, and dreams of glory that many in the regiment had hoped to win. Five to seven a day were laid beneath the earth, with the painful sound of the "Dead March" echoing in the ears of the living. Coffinless, with only a blanket shielding the corpse, three rifle shots marked the end of each deceased man. Following the previously mentioned formation, it was deemed proper to discharge all sick troopers that were considered entitled to such action. Subsequently, three hundred were discharged. These soldiers, plus the dead—nearly one hundred more—reduced the effective combatants of the "Bloody First" to less than five hundred.[13]

Thomas D. Tennery, a private in the 4th Regiment Illinois Volunteers, recorded ten deaths in his regiment between 25 August and September 19, 1846, with the comment that a soldier had to expect the continued presence of death. During this time the disease of mumps was spreading throughout his camp, and the hot weather increased the level of suffering. Theophilus Johnson, a campmate and friend of Tennery, caught the disease,[14] and finally died on November 8th at Camargo.[15]

At Camp Patterson in late September 1846, with the rainy season in full swing, the flat loam soil was a sea of mud. Life in such a miserable place made the troops delighted to leave. On the 24th they started for Matamoras, crossed several swamps and with exhaustion setting in, reached their destination. After being quartered overnight in a large brick building, the troops moved to the west side of town the next morning and set up camp on a beautiful sea of bluegrass.[17] The hospital at Matamoras had five or six rooms, large and spacious, where the sick were kept. Despite the space they were terribly crowded. There were insufficient beds and mattresses for all of the patients, and consequently, many a sick soldier had to sleep on the brick floor with only a blanket beneath them. And then, the care that they received, depended sorely on the whims of the nurses who were volunteers themselves.[18]

From Port Lavacca, during the latter part of September 1846, came the report that the surgeon there had reported 160 new sick cases as of the 23rd. Furthermore, that many of the men in the camp were without shoes, some without pants, or hats and coats. Nor had anyone seen any pay for his service.[19] Private Tennery noted in his diary, dated November 1st, that out of the 3rd and 4th Regiments Illinois Volunteers camped on the banks of the San Juan River, one to five men a day were being buried. Continuously referring to volunteers he knew,

Tennery remarked on the 11th that Kenny and Johnson, who had succumbed to measles, were buried in the first coffins that the soldiers had seen in Mexico.

Besides the constant threat of disease and death by its hand, the weather along the Rio Grande River seemed to play a role that was seldom beneficial. The wind was constantly stirring up clouds of sand and dust which hung over the San Juan Camp, getting into the bedding, food, and everything imaginable.[20] Then on the morning of 18 November, 1846, a sudden rain storm, accompanied by high winds, struck the camp with a vicious fury. Being a Wednesday, the weekly cleaning day, the tents had been collapsed, and all encountered considerable difficulty in getting them erected again. The rain was followed by a sudden drop in temperature which caused the men to huddle around the fires, and then just before morning the temperature dropped to a point just above freezing.[21] The next camp which Tennery found himself experiencing was near Rio del Tigre, and it was now mid-December, 1846. On the 18th he mentioned in his diary that James Perryman was unwell with the diarrhea, and on the 19th, that Job Clifton was dead. Then he made the recording that on the 22nd, between 12 noon and 2 p.m., it rained so hard that the tents had to be moved to the riverbank to escape the lake which had claimed the hastily evacuated camp site.[22]

In early September, 1846, in addition to those from the "Bloody First," between 250 and 300 volunteers were discharged from the Tennessee regiments due to ill health. The diseases in question were: congestive fever, inflammation of the bowels, chills and fever, and the measles. The latter was particularly deadly, being a completely different variety from that which was common in the United States.

The act of discharging the sick, so common during the Mexican War, was due to several factors: lack of proper medicines, the severity of the diseases, the severity and extremes of the climate, and the high rate of death among those who became ill. Lieutenant Eastman, a member of the Nashville Blues, reported to his loved ones at home, the unceasing efforts of Brig. General Pillow to ease the suffering of the sick.[23] During this fall of 1846 the Georgia Regiment had lost sixty-three men out of some 800 to sickness and accident, and at times, the sick list was so extensive that not more than three or four hundred could be mustered as an effective fighting force. A letter from one Major Forsyth of the Georgia Regiment seconded a previous description of the plight of the sick.

> A man gets sick and he is carried to the hospital with his blanket and his knapsack. Bed and bedding there are none, and, as the country is entirely destitute of lumber, bedsteads are not to be had. A blanket and the ground is therefore the couch upon which the volunteer lies

Around the Fires on a Cold Night

sick and dies, if he does not recover. If he dies the same blanket form his winding sheet and a coffin—plank is not to be had.

The major went on to state that in the two weeks following their departure from Matamoros, twenty-seven out of seventy sick men left behind had died. Another letter, this one from a Captain Thorton to the *Charleston Evening News*, recorded a figure of 700 Americans—three-fourths volunteers—being sick at Matamoros with dysentery, intestinal ulceration, and typhoid. The daily death rate was averaged at five per day.[25]

Great difficulty was experienced by the troops in receiving their pay, and consequently, their frequent destitute condition was aggravated (as was previously mentioned) by their own inability to purchase their necessities out of their own pockets. By late September 1846, Colonel Marshall's Kentucky Regiment was still waiting for some $75,000 dollars in back pay. And many of the men at the time, were without shoes and dressed in rags.[26] And out of the entire regiment 400 men were on the sick list.[27] Colonel Samuel R. Curtis, Commanding Officer of the 3rd Regiment Ohio Volunteers, reported in September that his regiment had 150 men on the sick list out of a force of 620. They had started with 780 men.[28] By late November 1846 it was estimated that some 1500 volunteers had found their graves on the banks of the Rio Grande River. During this same period, newly arrived regulars, according to the volunteers were rapidly being sent into the healthier interior regions.[29] In February 1847 smallpox broke out among the 2nd Regiment Pennsylvania Volunteers aboard the transports at Lobos Island. While the patients were restrained onboard the ship, the rest of the regiment landed on the island and set up camp.[30]

Although the volunteers had been in many camps that were inadequate, to say the least, probably the worst was Camp Misery near Jalapa. Sgt. J. Jacob Oswandel, of the 1st Regiment

Pennsylvania Volunteers, recorded that they arrived on the 21st of April, 1847, and halted in a field beyond the city. With no tents available, they were exposed during their stay to both rain and cold. The night of April 24/25th was especially cold and wet, and all of those with no shelter were soaked to the skin while trying to dry their blankets and clothes around the campfires. The air bristled with curses about the weather, the army, the regulars, and the government which had failed to adequately provide for their needs. Around noon on the 25th Oswandel and two companions, John Newman and Louis Bymaster, appropriated shingles and boards from a deserted ranch and erected a small hut.[31] Two days later, following another cold night, others followed their example by tearing down deserted buildings and creating crude shelters to sleep under.[32] On the 29th of April a storm of such magnitude that it destroyed nearby ranches and houses struck the camp. Oswandel and his companions had to hold on to their shanty to keep it from blowing away. And the rain came—and more rain, and more rain and more rain! Some of the crude shelters failed to withstand the wind, and others who had built their huts over holes dug in the ground, were flooded out. Many of the latter, who were asleep when the storm hit, had to be awakened to save them from drowning.[33] General Scott ordered the Surgeon General to examine the camp and the general condition of the troops. Accompanied by several other doctors, the Surgeon General immediately recognized the unhealthiness of Camp Misery, and recommended at once that the camp be evacuated without delay.[34]

Meanwhile, General Calwalader who was at Palo Alto, received a letter from the hospital at Matamoros on the subject of smallpox. Besides separating the sick from the healthy troops, the correspondence recommended vaccination, and revaccination, as the only sure methods of controlling the dread disease. Underlining the seriousness of the recommendation the General found enclosed some vaccination serum which he forwarded at once to his medical officer, Dr. Albert C. Renasey.[35] The latter, on the 4th of May, reported to the General in writing regarding the latest outbreak of measles. A dozen new cases had just occurred—and in accordance with instructions they had been confined to an area half a mile from the regular camp. The sick list was gradually decreasing, the doctor reported, and assigned the reasons to the good water, game, fish, and the general condition of the camp.[36]

Prior to their arrival in Mexico, the 2nd Regiment of the Missouri Rifles probably suffered more than any other unit at the hands of deadly disease. The ten companies which made up the regiment met at Vicksburg in early January 1847, without sufficient or appropriate clothing, expecting the government to outfit them. The majority were destined to be disappointed.[37] After spending the first couple of days in warehouses, the troops were moved to Camp McClung two and half miles north of the city. The site was a bad choice, being located on the low bank of the river and exposed to the north and west winds. Then the rains turned the ground, which was their bed, into a mass of mud and cold lakes. On the 10th the rain changed to sleet and hail, and the men huddled together in their tents and around smoking fires, seeking a bit of warmth to ease their miserable condition. The results were foredoomed: rheumatism, influenza, pneumonia, and a disease called the "cold plague."

In New Orleans their hopes for a better fate from disease and weather were quickly dashed. Encamped on the Battle Grounds just below the city, the men found the ground just as wet and the rain just as miserable as what they had experienced in Vicksburg. The sick men, hot with fever and wrapped in damp blankets, unintentionally caused their tents to become suffocating steam baths. The dying were eventually moved to beds of straw inside a dry building, while many others sought better quarters at their own expense. The more seriously ill were taken to Dr. Luzenberg's hospital; first by cabs to the river, there to be crammed into small tow boats, and then again stuffed into cabs, and then railroad cars—and finally, the hospital. During all of this transporting the screams of pain and agony recorded the suffering of the numerous patients. At the end of January 1847, when the regiment finally departed New Orleans, eighty men had to be left behind.

The regiment continued to suffer from diseases after their arrival in Mexico—even in the higher interior regions. Near Monterey the dreaded smallpox struck the already decimated unit. Dr. Love, the regimental doctor, provided on May 10, 1847, an accurate account of the situation.

> I have had a hard time with smallpox—over a hundred cases, including varioloid. We are getting nearly through with it—only about 25 cases of it in the hospital at this time, and nearly all of them convalescent. We have had only two new cases within six days. Vaccination has put a stop to it. The general health is improving. We have had two cases similar, in fact, the very same disease that troubled us at New Orleans. They were produced by exposure and imprudence—both proved fatal.[39]

General Scott's army also suffered from the normal camp diseases, and in addition, those troops in Vera Cruz had to contend with the onslaught of yellow fever.[40] The steam ship, *Massachusetts*, arrived in New Orleans from the Mexican city with 163 hospital cases on the 16th of June, 1847. Then, on the 21st, the steamer *James L. Day*, with 120 more yellow fever-stricken soldiers appeared off the mouth of the Mississippi River. Dr. Laut, stationed in Vera Cruz, reported that a great many soldiers in the city were unfit for duty due to illness; and he attributed many cases to yellow fever. Another doctor, Dr. Barnes, suggested that the yellow fever cases more closely approximated Remittent, and except for the brilliant red appearance of the eyes and black vomit just before death, it would not otherwise be diagnosed as yellow fever.[41]

The 1st Regiment Pennsylvania Volunteers had good quarters and food while encamped in the Castle de Perote between the 8th of May and the 3rd of July, 1847. However, the death rate remained high—primarily due to their previous exposure while at Camp Misery. The deaths between the 22nd and the 26th of June, which were all due to diarrhea, totaled twenty-six men.[42] The castle was later turned into a hospital. At one time it had 500 cases of diarrhea alone. The death casualties mounted so high that the Christian and military formalities were dispensed with entirely. The dead were wrapped in their blankets, temporarily placed in the dead-house, and a few days later—in their turn—carted to the burial ground and dumped two and three into holes with no headboard to mark their sacrifice.[43]

On his next march, which commenced on the 3rd of July, 1847, Oswandel recorded that the men had no tents and many were short of clothes. Rain and snow fell most of the time, and the exposure continued to thin the ranks.[44] After these troops had been assigned the duty of holding the City at Puebla, they found themselves confronted at one point with holding the city against an enemy force of over 3,000 troops. The volunteers had only 500 combat effectives—while over 1,500 more men were sick in the local army hospital.[45] The latter were referred to as the "diarrhea blues" and the "hospital rangers."[46] By January 1, 1848, Oswandel's regiment was only a shadow of what it had been the previous January. From nearly 1,000 men it had been reduced to approximately 400—and each company from about 100 to an average of 40 or 45 men. His own company had lost 52 men—only a very few to combat.[47]

General Scott's army, while at Puebla numbered 6,837 men, of which 1,017 were on the sick list. With the arrival of General Pillow's force the totals increased to 10,276 men with 2,215 unfit for duty due to illness. On August 6, 1847, General Pierce arrived and the army then numbered 12,776 combat soldiers, of whom, 3,100 were listed as ill. A large number of soldiers contracted diseases, especially during the summer months that proved fatal; although some lingered on for months and even years before succumbing. Brig. General Kearny, for example, died from a war-contracted disease at Jefferson Barrack on October 31, 1848; while General Persifar F. Smith clung to life until May 17, 1858, before his Mexican-contracted illness could claim its victim.[49] The total number that died from sickness, officers and men, totalled 10,900: more than seven times the numbers that died in—or later, as the result of one of the war's battles.[50]

Chapter 4

Heat of Battle

Brig. General Kearney on the 30th of June, 1846, departed Fort Leavenworth for Santa Fe, New Mexico, 873 miles away.[1] After stopping over at Fort Bent, the Army of the West reached Las Vegas, New Mexico, on the 15th of August without any opposition having been encountered. The oath of allegiance to the United States of America was administered to the people of the community that same day.[2]

Although General Kearney had received word that there would be no resistance offered, except to any small reconnoitering force which might proceed the main body,[3] Mexican troops were visible at the mouth of a canyon, six miles out of Las Vegas. By the time the American troops passed through, however, the enemy of 3,000 in all had vanished.[4] The governor was fleeing south toward Chihuahua,[5] Mexico, while the Americans continued their march toward Santa Fe. They reached the capital of New Mexico at 5 o'clock that afternoon. The date was August 18, 1846.[6]

Four hundred men, led by General Kearney, departed for California on the 25th of September mounted on mules.[7] Two hundred and five miles into the journey he learned that California had already been taken by Colonel Fremont, and consequently ordered three hundred of his troops to turn back.[8] Behind him he had left New Mexico in the hands of Charles Bent, his appointed governor, and Colonel Price, the military commander of the occupation forces. Under the colonel's authority there were four units: his own 2nd of Missouri Volunteers, Major M. Lewis Clark's battalion of horse artillery, and Captain Murphy's and Angney's companies of infantry.[9]

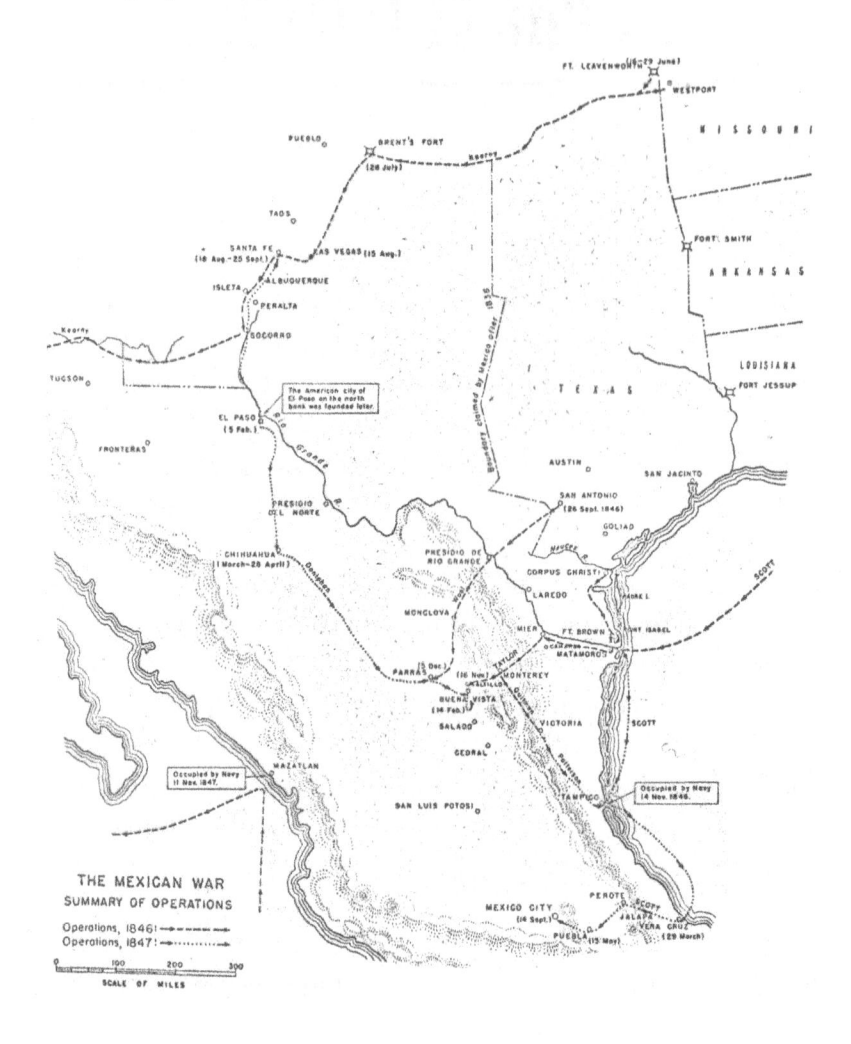

Colonel Doniphan and his Mormon volunteers had been ordered by General Kearney to march south along the Rio Grande River and join General Wool in Chihuahua, Mexico. In mid-December at Donal Ana, the colonel received news that the enemy was at El Paso, sixty miles south with four cannons and 700 mens. Around 3 p.m. on the 25th Doniphan's advance guard of 300 men halted their march for the day and started setting up camp. Then came the news that the enemy was moving toward them, and he was near at hand.[10] The resulting battle, known to the Americans as Brazito and by the Mexicans as Temascalitos, saw the Mexican force fleeing the field after Captain Reid and twenty mounted troopers had broken the fighting spirit of the enemy's cavalry, the Vera Cruz Dragoons. The casualties were seven volunteers wounded and none killed—the enemy, 43 killed and 15 wounded.

Subsequent to the enemy's evacuation of El Paso, the Mormons occupied it on the 27th. Then over a month later, on February 8th, after being informed that General Wool was not at Chihuahua, the American force set foot toward that city with 924 men and six cannons. At Sauy on the 27th Doniphan was informed that the enemy was entrenched at Sacramento Pass. The next day, after the main American force had halted three miles from the Mexican lines, reconnoitering patrols were sent out to probe the terrain and the enemy's defenses. They discovered that the pass was a plain with mountains on either side; that from the range to the west (on their right) a spur shot out which reduced the width of the pass to one and a half miles, and that on their left there was a deep arroyo. Between the spur and the arroyo there was a steep incline of about sixty feet.

The enemy force of 2,200 men, led by General Heredia and Governor Trias of New Mexico, waited for the attack as the American forces advanced to within one and a half miles—the cavalry even nearer. Then, at a signal, the entire American force swirled to the right and moved rapidly up the ridge beyond the left flank of the enemy's position. Although General Heredia tried to counter with his cavalry, this opening move by General Doniphan—a civilian at war—decided the outcome. Out of 924 volunteers able to fight, only 824 were actually engaged in the combat; but all shared in the victory.[11]

In San Antonio, Texas, during August 1846, General Wool issued Orders to Colonel Hardin to return with his regiment from the Presidio of the Rio Grande. The colonel, it was alleged, was so eager to engage his force in combat that he had marched south without orders. Now he was forced to return.[12] Besides Colonel Hardin's 1st Regiment Illinois Volunteers, Wool had under his command, Colonel Bissell's 2nd Regiment Illinois Volunteers, Colonel Yell's Arkansas Cavalry Regiment, Major Conneville's 6th Infantry Battalion, Captain William's company of Kentucky Volunteers, Captain Washington's artillery battery, and two squadrons of dragoons. The 6th Infantry Battalion and the two squadrons of dragoons—the 1st and the 2nd—were regular U.S. Army troops. Altogether, the general had 2,600 combat troops under his command.[13]

The army departed San Antonio on the 29th of September and entered Monclova on the 31st of October without resistance.[14] On January 30, 1847, General Wool had reported that Major Borland and 50 men of the Arkansas Cavalry, and Majors Gaines and Clay (Cassius M.) with 30 men of the Kentucky Cavalry, were captured at Encarnacion (45 miles from Saltillo) on the 23rd of the month by General Minion and a cavalry force of 500 troopers. And—without a shot being fired. They had disobeyed orders by proceeding further than authorized, and definitely demonstrated a lack of alertness. The general also reiterated the capture story of a small group of Kentucky volunteers who were engaged in consuming liquor at a Mexican ranche.[15]

While still encamped at Camargo, on the lower Rio Grande, General Taylor issued an order dated the 18th of August, 1846, which organized his army into three divisions. The 1st Division under Brig. General Twiggs, was composed of the 1st, 3rd, and 4th Regiments (infantry); the batteries of Webster, Bragg, and Ridgely; and the four companies of the 2nd Dragoons under May. In this division of regulars, Shiners' Volunteers and the Baltimore Battalion, later to be transferred to the Volunteer Division, were included. The division, including both the regulars and volunteers, totalled about 2,000 men. The 2nd Division was commanded by Brig. General Worth, and also contained both regulars and volunteers. Among the former there were the 5th, 7th, and 8th Infantry Regiments; Child's artillery battalion; plus the batteries of Mackall, Duncan, and the light troops of C. F. Smith. The volunteers were Blanchard's Company of Louisiana Volunteers, and McCulloch's and Gillispie's companies of mounted Texas Rangers. The total number of men comprising the division was approximately 1,800. The 3rd Division, known as the Volunteer Division, was under the command of Maj. General W. O. Bulter. The units consisted of the 1st Kentucky and 1st Ohio regiments in the 1st Brigade under Homer, and the 1st Tennessee and 1st Mississippi Rifles (Colonel Jefferson Davis) regiments in the 2nd Brigade under Quitman. The mounted troops were Henderson's (Governor of Texas) brigade of Texas rangers which were split into two regiments under Woods and Hays. The total division strength amounted to about 3,000 men, of which, nearly a 1,000 were Texas Rangers.[16]

The first major goal for this army was the enemy citadel of Monterey. Dawn of September 21, 1846, revealed General Taylor's forces in their initial assault:[17] the 1st Division on the right, the 2nd Division on the left, and the Volunteer Division commanding the center.[18] During the night of September 20th General Worth's division was camped west of the city at the base of the mountain dominated by Bishop's Palace. The following morning, minutes after darkness had fled the scene of the impending battle, the Americans were turning the point of a ridge and spotted a unit of Mexican cavalry charging down upon them. Captain Gillespie ordered his company to dismount, and as the enemy was about to charge into their ranks, the Rangers released a murderous volley of fire. Then McCulloch's company of Rangers and some regulars, charged into the enemy's midst in a hand-to-engagement. When the American artillery opened up on Mexican forces not actively engaged, but at the scene, the enemy broke, panicked, and hurriedly retreated. A devastating volley of rifle fire followed in their wake.[19]

The Volunteer Division formed behind a battery which was firing on the "Black Fort." The 1st Division, on the left, had moved on the eastern side of the city and formed up for the main assault. Since it was General Taylor's desire that the principal assault should be conducted by General Worth on the west side of the city, Lieut. Colonel Garland (Commander of the 1st Brigade), acting for the ailing General Twiggs, was ordered to make a strong demonstration in support. He was to carry the defenses on his front only if such could be done with ease. After the initial engagement by the 1st Division had resulted in a stalemate, the Volunteer Division was ordered to prepare for a hard fight; the Ohioans and Kentuckians on the right, and the Tennesseans and Mississippians on the left. With arrival of the 1st Tennessee in line, the order to attack rang out, and the ragged multi-colored troops surged forward to the assault. The Kentuckians remained in support of the artillery. Advancing through a continuous shower of shot and grape the volunteers were suddenly caught in a crossfire from three Mexican forts, and then, the order was heard to, "Halt and fire!" This gross error in leadership was instantly obeyed. As the men were being slaughtered the officers tried to rectify the error by ordering the charge renewed. With only a pause in the firing, their efforts were finally rewarded, as the enemy was killed, captured, or driven from their positions.[20] Colonel W. B. Campbell of the 1st Tennessee Volunteers,[21] thereafter known as the "Bloody First,"[22] wrote a letter in which he explained the reason for the unexpected crossfire in which the volunteers had been entrapped.

> My regiment went into action on the morning of the 21st, and was ordered to sustain some regulars who were said to be attacking a fort at one end of the city. When I arrived with them, no regulars were visible—they had filed to the right and taken shelter behind, and had got into the outskirts of town, so that my command was left exposed to the most severe discharge of artillery and musketry that was ever poured upon a line of volunteers. They bore the fire with wonderful courage, and rushed upon the fort and took it at the point of the bayonet.... My losses were 26 killed, 77 wounded, and 2 missing out of a total of 379.[23]

A member of the battalion, in a letter home, presented his observation of what occurred that morning to the Volunteer Division—of which his unit was now a part.

> On the morning of the 21st, around 8 o'clock, the battalion moved out of the cornfield toward an enemy fort in the face of heavy artillery and musket fire.[24] Then, despite sudden enfilading fire, the troops advanced to within a hundred yards of their goal. At that moment with success within their grasp,[25] the regulars (at least four companies) suddenly swerved to the right with Colonel Watson, the commanding officer of the Baltimore Battalion following suit.[26] This exposed their flank even more, and because not all men understood the order, the necessary momentum was lost.[27]

Although they had gained the edge of the city, militarily they were on a dead end street,[28] with three batteries of the enemy within 100 yards and thousands of riflemen on the roof tops, behind the barricade at the end of the street, and at every intersection in between.[29] The fire was so intense that the dead, both men and horses, became a carpet upon which the living were forced to walk.[30] Following Colonel Watson's slow advance, which only secured about 50 yards, Colonel Garland reluctantly gave the order to retire.[31] The troops then retreated to the shelter of Fort Teneria, which had been seized by a battalion of the 4th Infantry U.S. Army, and General Auitman's brigade of the 1st Mississippi and 1st Tennessee Volunteers. Although the leadership had failed at the critical moment, the men could hold their heads high, for their bravery was not to be questioned. "We will fight with brave Baltimoreans," was the pledge heard throughout the ranks.[32]

The next morning around 9 a.m., September 22nd, Colonel Garland's command was relieved from its occupation of Fort Teneria by General Quitman's brigade. The day was one of waiting, with the dodging of enemy shot, shell, and grape, the primary activity.[33] Another irritation was the wet and dreary weather which hung over the city. In the afternoon the men were greeted by the sight of General Worth's troops securing the heights on the city's west side and storming Bishop's Palace.[35]

Early on the 23rd General Quitman gave orders that a portion of his command was to occupy Fort Diablo,[36] a triangular redoubt,[37] which had been abandoned during the night. Later in the morning the general, taking advantage of his orders to seize advantages as he saw fit, issued instructions to Colonel Davis and Lieut. Colonel Anderson to lead two companies of the 1st Mississippi Rifles and the 1st Tennessee in an attack. After the fighting had commenced the remainder of the brigade, all that could be spared, were thrown into the battle.[38] After penetrating deep into the city, General Taylor ordered General Henderson to take Wood's regiment of Texas Rangers and support the efforts of the attacking force. With cries of "Goliad and Alamo,"[39] the rangers fought from house to house with an unnerving fury. In this type of warfare the Texans had no equals, and by late afternoon, with the Mississippians and Tennesseans at their side, had fought to within a hundred and fifty yards of the central plaza. Finally, because of concern that the troops were entering the range of their own artillery, and with ammunition near exhaustion, the troop were halted while the light artillery was brought forward. When it was determined that the enemy positions were too strong, the men were ordered back to their positions of that morning.[40]

A volunteer from Louisiana, one S. D. Allis, wrote to an uncle about the part that Blanchard's Louisiana Company had played in seizing Bishop's Palace. The volunteers attacked and seized three enemy batteries which were located on the summits of several steep hills; so steep that a wrong step would have resulted in a fall of several hundred feet. Then in the attack on the castle itself they hugged the earth within 200 yards of the walls for five hours. Finally they charged with the 7th Infantry at their side and took the castle.[41]

On the 24th, at 12 a.m., four companies of Texas Rangers and two of artillery were instructed to storm the height where a nearby fort was located. The 7th Infantry and the Louisiana boys were ordered by Colonel Persifer F. Smith (who commanded the brigade containing the 5th and the 7th) to charge from the flanks. The charge became a mad desperate race to see which command would penetrate the fort first. Although it was close, the 5th made it first; the Mexicans fleeing out the other side.[42] On the later side of the afternoon General Ampudial, commander of the Mexican forces in that area, capitulated.[43]

From a disbanded Louisiana regiment several volunteers refused to go home. The prime example was that of Captain Smith of New Orleans and Lieutenant Price from Natchez who walked from Camargo to Monterey in six days. On the last day they had walked sixteen miles, and upon reaching the city had borrowed rifles from the sick and joined the 3rd and 4th Infantries. Later they fought with the 1st Mississippi Rifles, and then on the 23rd with the Texas Rangers in house-to-house combat. Neither received a scratch.[44]

An order, dated December 10, 1846, was delivered to the Baltimore Battalion directing the unit to be transferred from the 4th Brigade of the 1st Division to the 2nd Brigade (Brig. General Quitman) within the 3rd Division. The other units were the 1st Regiment Mississippi Rifles, the 1st Regiment Georgia Volunteers, and the 1st Regiment Tennessee Volunteers.[45] Then on the 18th the 1st and 2nd Tennessee Regiments were joined to form one brigade, while the 1st Mississippi Rifles, the 1st Georgia, and the Baltimore Battalion, formed a second brigade. Together they constituted a new volunteer division under Brig. General Quitman.[46] This division captured Victoria, capital of the State of Tamaulipas, on the 29th of the month, and in the moment of victory, paid honor to its brave Baltimore Battalion by hoisting its flag to the top of the State House.[47]

By December of 1846 the preparations for opening a new front at Vera Cruz had stripped General Taylor of all his regular infantry, leaving the three batteries commanded by Captains Bragg, Washington, and W. T. Sherman, and the dragoon (cavalry) force under Lieut. Colonel May as the only regular army units.[48] With this predominately volunteer army, General Taylor became aware in the middle of February 1847 that enemy forces—desiring to take advantage of his reduced manpower—had commenced moving in his direction. Subsequently he had his small force fall back to a pass near the town of Buena Vista.[49] There he waited; on the 20th his intelligence informed him that the enemy had advanced to Encarnacion, thirty miles from his front.[50] In their selected battle field positions, General Taylor's force of 4,759 men awaited Santa Anna's army of 20,000 Strong.[51] As the two armies stood facing each other on the evening of the 22nd the enemy threw out light troops on the mountain side—

the American left—in an attempt to outflank the Gringos. The attempt failed.[52]

Taylor's troops commanded position of substantial strength: to the right of their lines, they were protected by a valley which was chopped up in a pattern of numerous gullies, and on the left, there existed a series of steep ridges and ravines extending far back toward the mountains. In essence, the terrain prohibited the effective use of artillery and cavalry by the Mexican forces, and greatly nullified Santa Anna's numerical superiority in infantry. General Taylor reported his initial disposition of forces in the following manner.

> Captain Washington's battery of the 4th Artillery was posted to command the road, while the 1st and 2nd Illinois Regiments under Colonels Hardin and Bissell, each eight companies (to the latter was attached Captain Conner's company of Texas Volunteers), and the 2nd Kentucky under Colonel McKee, occupied the crests of the ridges on the left and in the rear. The Arkansas and Kentucky regiments of cavalry, (commanded by Colonels Yell and H. Marshall) occupied the extreme left near the base of the mountain, while the Indiana Brigade commanded by Brig. General Lane (composed of the 2nd and 3rd regiments under Colonel Bowles and Lane), the Mississippi Riflemen under Colonel Davis, the squadrons of the 1st and 2nd Dragoons under Captain Steem and Lieut. Colonel May, and the light batteries of Captain Shermen and Bragg, 3rd Artillery, were held in reserve.[54]

On the evening of the 22nd General Taylor proceeded with the Mississippi Rifles and a squadron of the 2nd Dragoon to Saltillo, just north of Buena Vista, to ensure the safety of his munitions and stores.[55] Prior to full daylight on the 23rd, with

General Taylor yet to return, the enemy commenced his assault with a savage attack on the American left. The fighting soon resulted in an envelopment of the Arkansas and Kentucky cavalry regiments by Mexican light troops with the aide of an artillery battery. And although outnumbered six to one, the volunteers clung tenaciously to their mountain spur terrain. At the same time Santa Anna threw a large body of infantry and cavalry against the front held by the 2nd Illinois and Indiana Regiments with O'Brien's battery in support. Occupying the left and upper part of the huge plateau, this force under Brig. General Lane, was facing possible liquidation by this enemy force with its eight-pounder battery. The firing of artillery and muskets and the smoke and noise became extremely intense, and then, the men of the 2nd Indiana and O'Brien's battery found themselves being enfiladed by cannister and grape from their left flank. Suddenly the 2nd Indiana broke, and it's unclear

TABLE 1: THE AMERICAN ARMY AT BUENA VISTA

REGIMENTS/MISC. UNITS	COMPANIES
2nd Regiment Kentucky Volunteers	10
1st Regiment Mississippi Rifles	8
2nd Regiment Indiana Volunteers	10
3rd Regiment Indiana Volunteers	8
1st Regiment Illinois Volunteers	8
2nd Regiment Illinois Volunteers	8
Texas Volunteers	1
Arkansas Volunteer Cavalry	10
Kentucky Volunteer Cavalry	7
Texas Rangers	1
3 batteries regular artillery/2 squadrons regular cavalry	453 men

whether their movement was only aided by Colonel Bowles' order to fall back, or set in motion by it. Efforts by General Lane and other officers were of no avail as the regiment, now a mob of civilians, fled in disorderly array from the field. O'Brien and his battery stood their ground until the last moment and then fell back in good order.[56]

The 2nd Kentucky with Bragg's battery and the 1st Illinois with Washington's battery were rushed up from the rear and managed to check the onrushing tide in their immediate fronts. Behind the fleeing troops however, the pursuing enemy cavalry was encircling the Arkansas and Kentucky men still battling General Ampudia's forces in the foothills. The commander of these forces ordered his men to retreat in order to prevent being cut off.

At this juncture General Taylor arrived on the field and ordered Jefferson Davis to take his riflemen forward and halt the enemy forces sweeping down from the mountains.[57] Passing through the ranks of the fleeing Indiana troops the Mississippi men attempted to halt their flight, but to no avail. Colonel Davis, addressing his men, is alleged to have shouted contemptuously, "There is a mass of men behind which you can take shelter and securely form!"[58] The commander of the 2nd Indiana, Colonel Bowles, and some of his men, joined the Mississippi regiment and fought bravely the entire day. Later some of the 2nd Indiana assisted in defending the train and depot at the town of Buena Vista. The remainder, whoever, could not be rallied to fight further that day.[59]

As the Mexicans approached the Mississippi Rifles held their fire, restraining their impulse to shot; then the enemy came within range. Finally, when General Ampudia's troops were almost on top of them, they fired a point-blank volley of devastating death which created a wall of enemy dead along the entire front. Then the Rifles leaped down into the ravine in their immediate front, reloaded, and charged up the opposite side where they poured a second volley into the enemy troops. Then a third volley, and still another—the enemy halted, confused—then panic became their master and they fled for safety. At this point the 3rd Indiana came up and reinforced the Mississippi Rifles. On the extreme left the Arkansas and Kentucky cavalry units, reinforced by the 2nd Dragoons and a squadron of the 1st managed to beat off General Torrejon and forced his troops to fall back.[60]

A new body of the enemy, 1,000 cavalry and 2,500 infantry, came charging down from the upper reaches of the great plateau toward Colonels Davis and Lane with their 1,000 men. The Mississippi Rifles and the 3rd Indiana were ordered into V-shaped angle with the mouth awaiting the enemy assault. The Mexican cavalry, as it approached, slowed to a trot, hoping to draw the American fire and then ride them down before they could reload. The volunteers—with bated breath—waited. The Mexican horsemen slowed to a walk as they entered the angle. Suddenly one thousand rifles roared, and Sherman's battery barked out its hell of grape and cannister. The enemy milled around in panic, trampling their own dead and wounded in their fearful search for escape. A white flag appeared suddenly behind the rear ranks of the Mexican forces—the firing ceased, and the enemy fled the battlefield. It had been a ruse to save the Mexican troops, and it had worked.[61]

Having reoccupied nearly all of the morning positions, General Taylor instructed all artillery to concentrate on the center of the line where he believed the next attack would strike. With all units in the battle line the Kentucky and Illinois troops moved into the ravines where the majority of the enemy was forming. Encountering about 12,000 Mexican soldiers, the cream of the enemy force, the volunteers were forced back into a branch ravine. As Mexican cavalry poured in on them, enemy infantry delivered a murderous fire from the banks overhead. The volunteers battled their way down the ravine toward the road where Washington's battery was located, the fire of the latter driving the enemy off. The volunteer's loses were between 200 and 300 men.[62]

While a portion of Santa Anna's army was trying to destroy the volunteers trapped in the ravine, the main column bore down on O'Brien's three light artillery pieces. Cut off from the rest of the American army the battery fought furiously, refusing to surrender. In the rear the Mississippi Rifles and the 3rd Indiana, supported by cavalry and artillery, were struggling through ravines and over rough terrain to reach O'Brien and his men. As Bragg and Sherman, Davis and Lane, struggled through the last ravine prior to gaining the plateau, O'Brien's men discharged their cannons at point-blank range and then abandoned the guns. The rescue arrived and the Mexicans were hit by two batteries in their front while Washington's poured in a crossfire, and on their flanks the two volunteer regiments killed and maimed with a fierce rifle and musket fire. As holes appeared in the ranks of the enemy, and his forward movement slowed, the Americans seized the offensive and forced him off the field of battle.[63]

During the course of the night, it was discovered that the enemy had retreated to Agua Nueva, and since the American forces were greatly inferior in numbers, General Taylor elected not to pursue.[64] S. Compton Smith recorded approximately 400 Americans wounded and 300 killed; while Mexican losses were 2,500 killed and wounded, and 4,000 missing.[65]

The government had become aware by the fall of 1846 that the military successes of the United States had not convinced the Mexican authorities of the folly of continued resistance. Consequently, it was decided to occupy various ports along the Gulf of Mexico and to land an army at Vera Cruz for a direct thrust at the nation's capital of Mexico City. The line of the Sierra Madre would become a holding action only.[66] On the 9th of March, 1847, an American Army under the command of Maj. General Scott was landed near Vera Cruz, Mexico. By the 22nd the city had been completely invested, and five days later on the 27th the municipal authorities surrendered to the rule of the occupation forces.[67]

General Scott's army consisted of over 12,000 men in three divisions under Generals Worth, Twiggs, and Patterson. Brig. General Worth had Blanchard's Louisiana and William's Kentucky companies as the only volunteers in an otherwise regular manned 1st Division. The 2nd Division, under Brig. General Twiggs, was composed entirely of regular troops. The 3rd Division, under Brig. General Patterson, was entirely a volunteer force and consisted of the following regiments: the 1st and 2nd Tennessee, the 1st and 2nd Pennsylvania, units of the 3rd and 4th Illinois, the 1st New York, the 1st South Carolina, the 1st Georgia, and the 1st Alabama. Later, a unit of Tennessee cavalry was added to the division.[68]

On the 8th of April, 1847, the 2nd Division departed Vera Cruz as the spearhead of the army in its march on Mexico City. On the 9th the volunteer brigades of Generals Shields and Pillow likewise departed, followed on the 14th by General Quitman's brigade. On the 13th General Twiggs had sent a message back to army headquarters that the enemy was massed just beyond the hamlet of Plan del Rio. Thus the stage was set for the Battle of Cerro Gordo.

On the night of the 17th, under exceedingly difficult conditions, four companies of the New York Volunteers [69] assisted in dragging and lifting a 24-pounder breaching gun, with two 24-pound howitzers, over the newly cut road to a ridge which overlooked the southern flank and rear of Cerro Gordo. These artillery pieces, with the coming of dawn, would have the enemy batteries within their range.[70]

The plan of attack called for Colonel Harney and his 3rd Infantry, a company of sappers and miners, supported by the 1st Artillery, to storm the heights of Cerro Gordo. Colonel Riley, commanding the 2nd Infantry and the 4th Artillery, was to move forward on the right flank of the hill in order to block reinforcements while gaining the Jalapa Road in the rear. General Shields, with his brigade of volunteers, was assigned the role of sustaining the assault or to advance on the extreme right and seize the enemy battery in the highway northwest of Cerro Gordo, depending on how the battle developed. General Pillow was under orders to attack, or threaten, as circumstances dictated, the Mexican fortifications on their right flank which commanded the main road.[71]

The next morning, the 18th of April, the batteries which had so laboriously been hauled to the heights south of Cerro Gordo, opened the battle with destructive effect on the main portion of the enemy's positions. Colonel Harney and his troops fought their way up the steep slopes through a continuous hail of bullets and grape shot. Without a pause they reached and seized their objective. Colonel Riley's force, advancing at the same time on the right, participated in the successful offensive.[72] General Shields, with his New Yorkers under Colonel Burnett, and the 3rd and 4th Illinois under Foreman and Baker,[73] led his brigade in a charge upon the enemy's headquarters, plus a battery nearby. The General fell, severely wounded by grape,[74] and Colonel Baker took over the command, urging the men on. Riley's troops reached the road at about the same junction, and as the last fortification was stormed the enemy took to his heels;[75] Santa Anna himself leaving his coach and fleeing on a mule.[76]

When the army departed Puebla (near Cerro Gordo) on the next leg of its advance to Mexico City, it had been reorganized into four divisions. The first three were regular troops under Generals Worth, Twiggs, and Pillow; the other one, the 4th Division, was comprised mainly of inexperienced volunteers. Commanded by Brig. General Quitman, it consisted of the 2nd Regiment Pennsylvania Volunteers, Watson's U.S. Marines, Steptoe's field battery, the 1st Regiment New York Volunteers, and the 1st Regiment South Carolina Volunteers. The latter two were now commanded by General Shields as a brigade.[77]

Following the Battle of Cerro Gordo, Shields and his volunteers (the Carolina boys having replaced the Illinois volunteers) continued to distinguish the volunteer soldier. On the night of August 19th his brigade and three others found themselves in the hamlet of Contreras near Mexico City, about a half mile closer to the capital than the enemy's entrenched positions. Shields arrived on the scene after the plan of attack had already been conceived, and consequently, although the senior officer present, waived his right to command and instead assumed the anchor duty of the impending action. With his brigade he was to hold the hamlet against an enemy force ten times his own, and in doing so block their retreat to the capital if the plan was successful.[78]

Early in the morning the attack was launched, and within twenty minutes every portion of the enemy's defenses had been overwhelmed; the Mexican troops fleeing over the Magdalena Bridge where they were cut to ribbons by the crossfire of General Shield's command. The Mexican force had been practically annihilated by this action. That afternoon the Battle of Churubusco, which included the Church of San Pablo, and with the participation of the infamous San Patricio Battalion, ended in another American victory.[79]

At Chapultepec, on September 13th, General Quitman's volunteer division made the assault on the series of strong fortifications at the southeast approaches while General Pillow's troops attacked from the west. General Shields moved across the low and marshy ground with his New York and South Carolina volunteers, followed by the 2nd Pennsylvania. A storm of dense musket fire, grape shot, and cannister, ripped into their ranks, splattering the living with blood and gore. The survivors kept charging, with the South Carolinians being the first to reach the wall. Seizing picks and crowbars the troops breached the wall and assaulted the Mexican troops on the other side with the cold steel of the bayonet. The New Yorkers and Pennsylvanians reached the wall at a different point, and after forcing their way through in similar fashion, assisted in seizing the objective.

There were two roads leading to Mexico City from Chapultepec, the most direct being by way of the Tacubaya Causeway on which is situated the fortified Garita de Belen. Quitman's troops were under orders to advance only to a point from which they could demonstrate against this enemy stronghold. But seized by the same emotional bravery that drove his volunteers the General urged his men forward, and they charged through the enemy's deadly fire to seized the defenses of the Garita de Belen and on into the streets of Mexico City. Entering the city the same day, September 14, 1847,[80] General Scott made this announcement:

> Let me present to you the civil and military Governor of the City of Mexico, Maj. General John A. Quitman. I appoint him at this instant. He has earned this distinction and shall have it.[81]

The total number of troops who served in the war with Mexico was approximately 100,000—26,690 regular United States Army troops including a few hundred Marines, and 56,925 volunteers; the remainder being in the navy, commissariat, and transportation departments. Out of these numbers 120 officers and 1,400 enlisted men were killed in or died as a result of battle. Added to those numbers the 10,000 deaths from disease, plus those disabled and ruined in health, and the final tally reached the figure of 25,000 casualties. The cost reached a level between 130 and 160 million dollars.[82] On May 29, 1848, Maj. General Bulter, who had succeeded General Scott in command of the occupation forces, issued Oder #212, which declared the war at an end.[83]

Chapter 5

Opinions: Past and Present

The ill feeling which existed between the professional soldiers of the United States Army and the civilian volunteers during the Mexican War was nothing new in the annals of American warfare; it can be traced from colonial times to the present day. It is based, at any point in history, mainly on the opinion—negative and incomplete—which the professional soldier has of the amateur, the volunteer, and of the part-time soldier, the reserve. In an article published before General Scott's landing at Vera Cruz, Mexico, it was stated that such an invasion of Mexico's interior regions must rest primarily on the responsible shoulders of the regular troops if success was to be guaranteed. The basis for this statement was assigned to the corresponding discipline and fighting ability of the Mexican Troops which would have to be overcome; implying in this statement that the volunteers failed to measure up in the midst of battle. In the same breath it was determined that for defense of the homeland or beyond the reaches of civilization—for example in the American west—the individualistic volunteers were in the proper environment. To support these claims the correspondence of George Washington was enlisted.[1]

From Matamoros in August of 1846, a letter—probably written by a regular soldier—further supported the supremacy of the regular troops over the volunteers in its emphasis on the primary military element of discipline. It was alleged that the people of Matamoros were delighted to have the regular soldier as guests so as to ensure the security of themselves and their families. The volunteers were supposedly of the belief that a state of war meant a license to engage in whatever negative behavior they desired against the native population. The letter also contained the belief that one good charge would be the extent of the volunteers' combat participation.[2] Although the volunteers' willingness to fight could never be definitely ascertained prior to combat—or consistency of his nerves while in combat—the Battle of Monterey laid the aforementioned insult to rest in an early grave. The Texans demonstrated their bravery and sharply honed fighting skills as they fought fiercely from house to house, and street to street, with rifle and cannon, and often in hand-to-hand combat. The claim of the Mississippi and Tennessee regiments to equality with the Texans is supported by the fact, that of all the volunteer units, theirs suffered the heaviest losses as they fought their way into the heart of the city.[3] The 1st Tennessee, which was the first regiment to storm the fort, had fifty-four casualties (twenty-seven of whom were killed) out of a total volunteer force of three hundred and seventy-nine men.

Another volunteer unit which received special praise was the Baltimore Battalion. General Twiggs was overheard stating that this battalion had conducted itself in a heroic manner which was not excelled by any other unit in the army.[5] Colonel Watson, commanding officer of the battalion, said just before he was struck down, "Who will dare say now that American volunteers cannot be depended upon in any fight."[6]

The 22nd and 23rd of September, 1846, during the battle for Monterey saw most of the volunteers without food and, during the bad weather on the night of the 22nd, without blankets or other cover.[7] The food had been spoiled by the rains, although some of the men did have a little raw corn to eat. This deprivation was borne in a manly manner by the majority of the volunteers.[8] One volunteer, a Major Giddings, related in a letter to a friend how a number of regulars commented on the bravery of the volunteers following the surrender of Monterey. The compliment was a backhanded one in that the volunteer's camp habits and conduct was criticized at the same time.[9]

Since the fighting in the streets of Monterey forced the troops into many small groups, the individualism of the volunteers was positively manifested in many acts of personal heroism.[10] Following the battle General Bulter was left with his division as the occupying force, a duty for which the volunteers were most ill-suited due to the lack of adequate discipline within their ranks. One of these regiments, the 2nd Regiment Kentucky Volunteers, forwarded a warning to General Taylor against denying them a role in any future battles. Although such a denial had not been issued, they saw their present role as an indication of a future development, as an implied criticism of their conduct in the Battle of Monterey, and consequently threatened to mutiny if the general denied them a future fighting role.[11]

The Battle of Buena Vista was unique among all the battles that eventually came under the heading of the Mexican War: for on this one occasion, the primary role belonged to the civilian volunteers. Every last infantry soldier was a volunteer, and only one regiment, the Mississippi Rifles under Colonel Jefferson Davis, had previously been in combat; and the cavalry contained a ratio of four volunteers—with no previously combat experience in the Mexican War—to every regular mounted soldier. Only the artillery batteries were entirely of regular U.S. Army troops.[12] In giving the regulars their due, it has to be acknowledged that several regiments were commanded by volunteers who were West Point graduates: Lieut. Colonel Henry Clay Jr., of the Kentucky volunteers (who was killed during the battle), Colonel William R. McKee of the same regiment, Colonel Jefferson Davis of the Mississippi Rifles, and Colonel Humphrey Marshall of the Kentucky Cavalry.[13] In fact, the *Daily Picayune* of New Orleans took the ridiculous position of declaring that the victory was due to the west Point graduates and the U.S. Army officers and men of the artillery batteries.[14]

The units which received the highest praise were those of the Mississippi and Illinois volunteers, while the scorn of all was cast on the 2nd Indiana which had broke in panic on the 23rd. Courage, among the ranks of the volunteers, was the general rule throughout this battle.[15] The nature of the terrain caused the battle to develop into a series of seemingly unrelated and separate engagements, which allowed the united force of individualism to exercise its maximum effect on the fighting and emerge in the end as a great victory.[16]

The opinions concerning the abilities and courage, plus the habits, of the volunteers varied from one extreme position to the other. Captain E. Kirby Smith, U.S. Army, whose dislike of the volunteers was intense, arrived in Camargo, Mexico, around the 5th of October, 1846, where he received orders from General Patterson to organize an escort for the supply train headed for Monterey. Upon inquiry he discovered that he had seventy-one regulars and one hundred twelve volunteers available, of which about twenty were officers. His force, with which he was anything but pleased, he described in a letter written from Monterey after his arrival:

> I wrote you from Camargo, which place I left on the 15th in command of my ragged battalion; it was a serious

task to control such a heterogeneous body composed as it was of volunteers from different commands, sneaks and invalids of all the regular companies who were left behind at this place when the army advanced.[17]

Continuing with his comments, Smith stated that his unit was roused out on the morning of the 8th of January, 1847, with orders to depart the community of Saltillo. The local inhabitants were fearful of their lives since only volunteers were remaining. It was alleged that these same troops had behaved in barbaric ways toward them in the past. On the 10th Captain Smith's command passed through the little village of Los Muertos, which they recalled had been a community of happy people. This time, however, the people were not there. The volunteers had been! The buildings and shrubbery were in assorted states of ruin, and the ground was littered with the carcasses of dead and rotting animals.[18] Arriving at Punta Aguada on the 16th they discovered another recently created "ghost town." Like the hand of death the volunteers had been quite thorough in their plague-like destruction.[19]

Captain Smith is on record as saying that it was fortunate that there were no volunteers in the battle on May 9, 1846, near Matamoros.[20] He considered himself very lucky that he was in a unit of all regulars under General Taylor.[21] On the 5th of May, 1847, he wrote in a letter that the volunteers were expensive, barbaric, and undependable in battle; that their approach was dreaded by the Mexican civilians like a plague (while the regulars were looked upon as friends); that portions of them had fled in every battle they had fought in including Buena Vista. And furthermore, that these opinions were held by all regular soldiers and a large portion of the volunteer officers. Apparently Captain Smith never heard of the "San Patricio Battalion," or what is more likely, that he elected to ignore the obvious. He placed himself in the position of either being extremely naive, or a liar, by his own words:[22]

> The first instance is yet to occur in this war in which a regular has abandoned his post or been defeated. Portions of the volunteers have fought gallantly, but when they will fight, and when they won't, can only be determined by experiment.[23]

The opinions of Lieutenant Thomas Williams of the 4th Artillery, and Major Luther Giddings of the Ohio Volunteers show even further the extent of the controversy over the merits of the volunteer soldier. Williams complained that the volunteers always shared the credit, despite the fact that the regulars had, and without complaint, shouldered the entire load. The merits of the volunteers had been established by those vote-seeking individuals back home. The volunteers are, he concluded, "Useless, useless… expensive, wasteful…good for nothing." Major Giddings, on the other hand, saw the volunteers in the emotional cast of young Greek gods going off to do battle with giant Latin warriors.[24] Young George B. McClellan, fifteen years later to become a center of controversy himself during the Civil War, agreed completely with Captain Smith and Lieutenant Williams.[25]

In the official reports which were submitted by all officers following the Battle of Buena Vista, praise was high for the volunteer soldier. At the same time the fact cannot be ignored: that there were some whose conduct was shameful. Brig. General Lane gave special praise to Colonel Jefferson Davis (subsequently to become the President of the Confederacy during the Civil War) and his Mississippi Riflemen for their bravery and fierce fighting. He was of the opinion that regular veteran troops could not have done better than the volunteers had done on that field.[26]

Colonel Davis recalled in his report that his unit had reached the field after the battle had commenced and saw the horrifying sight of an American regiment fleeing panic-stricken from the field. That he took is regiment through their fleeing ranks in an effort to plug the line, and that he pleaded with them to turn back—but to no avail.[27]

Captain T. W. Sherman, 3rd Artillery, commanding Light Company E, had commented on the volunteers in his report with words of praise. The enemy had charged the right side of the line, where the Mississippi and 3rd Indiana, plus his batteries, stood rooted in their path. Despite the heavy fire the Mississippi regiment proved themselves the equal of the best of regular troops.[28]

The volunteers were all-convinced that the regulars were the favorites of the high command, and interpreted all existing evidence as sustaining that belief. Colonel William Campbell of the 1st Regiment Tennessee Volunteers stated several complaints concerning the regular troops. He claimed that the regulars were not concerned with justice being given to the volunteers, that they regretted the success of the volunteer forces at Buena Vista, and, that they received all the comforts and praise while the volunteers did without. He concluded by declaring that only danger to his country and home would compel him to ever again serve as a volunteer.[29]

One young volunteer wrote that he was terribly afraid the first time he was subjected to combat. But, upon looking around he saw that all were running toward the enemy, and that he couldn't stomach the thought of being the first to run in the opposite direction.[30] Another volunteer wrote from Camp Belknap in July of 1846, that he had enlisted to fight, but instead found himself with time on his hands. He alleged that this was due to General Taylor's belief that one regular soldier was worth five civilian volunteers.[31]

General Taylor's opinion of the volunteer soldier was revealed in a series of letters and statements during the course of the war. One of the recipients of his letter was Surgeon R. C. Wood, U.S. Army, of Fort Polk, Texas. The volunteer system, the general wrote, was defective, and mismanaged by those who are primarily

Major General Zachary Taylor

interested in their own political advancement. He insisted that the volunteers were unsuited for invading a foreign country and should be utilized only for defending the United States in accordance with the provisions of the Constitution;[32] that if the war continued much longer Congress would have to increase the size of the regular army as the volunteers were too inclined to leave as soon as their time had expired.[33] Furthermore, unless they were blended with older veterans, they seem to contact every disease that was known to mankind.[34]

Concerning the conduct of the volunteers during the battle of Monterey, General Taylor had high praise, particularly for the Mississippi and Tennessee regiments and the Texas riflemen.[35] Later on, following the occupation of that city, the general received complaints from Governor Morales about excesses being committed by the volunteers against Mexican civilians. The charges proved to be true. Consequently, the general promised that the volunteers would be removed from the city.[36]

The New England States had not received any request for troops, but the soldiers in Mexico heard rumors that Massachusetts was sending a regiment anyways. Soon after this unit had landed at Matamoros news begin to filter to the interior of the outrages being committed by the New England volunteers. These outrageous acts, which unfortunately were true, caused many Massachusetts volunteers to leave their regiment and join other units upon reaching Monterey.[37] When General Taylor's army was being drained of manpower for General Scott's offensive against the Mexican heartland, he made the following remark to his Adjutant General:

> Major Bliss, the next requisition Scott makes upon us, send him that infernal Massachusetts regiment. I have no need of them—and he is quite welcome to them.

"And I am sure, General," replied the Major, "we shall then no longer be troubled with his requisitions."[38]

For the volunteers of Buena Vista he had nothing but high praise. In his report of March 6, 1847, to the Secretary of War, he commenced his comments with the following word:

> I perform a grateful duty in bringing to the notice of the government the general good conduct of the troops. Exposed for successive nights without fires to the severity of the weather, they were ever prompt and cheerful to the discharge of every duty, and finally displayed conspicuous steadiness and gallantry in repulsing at great odds, a disciplined force. While the brilliant success achieved by their arms releases me from the painful necessity of specifying many bad conduct before the enemy, I feel an increased obligation to mention particular corps and officers, whose skill, coolness, gallantry in trying situations and under a continued and heavy fire, seem to merit particular notice.

He then mentioned particular officers and units, bestowing favorable comments on the Kentucky and Arkansas cavalry regiments, the 1st and 2nd Illinois, the 2nd Kentucky, the spy company of Texas Rangers under McCulloch, and as previously mentioned, the 1st Regiment Mississippi Rifles. His praise of this latter regiment and their commander, Colonel Jefferson Davis, had no limit![39]

And yet, he was anything but pleased over the behavior of the volunteer soldiers while in camp or town. He informed the Adjutant General of the U.S. Army that he had attempted by every means possible to halt their barbaric behavior, but that the undisciplined nature of a large portion of their rank and file had perpetuated such conduct. He stated, "With scarcely an exception, and with none in the latter class of offenses (acts of violence against civilians), these have been confined to the volunteer troops."[40]

Further south, General Scott wrote the Secretary of War from Camp Washington near Vera Cruz. Reporting on the landing of the troops, the general remarked that the brunt of the skirmishing, as of that date, had been handled by the volunteer units in a very competent manner. This remark was seconded by Maj. General Patterson's report of March 14th, in which he stated that no man or unit in his volunteer division should be ashamed, but to the contrary, proud of their behavior.[41]

General Scott had years previously expressed his basic opinion of volunteer soldiers while fighting Seminole Indians in Florida. In requesting more troops from the government during that campaign he had stated that the fighting required "good troops—not volunteers."[42] Prior to leaving Vera Cruz he wrote the Secretary of War regarding the subject of volunteer soldiers. He believed that the twelve-months volunteers would give him trouble as the end of their service approached. And in this prediction he was correct.[43] On the 15th of April General Scott informed the Secretary that one Louisiana company was requesting to be discharged the following month, as it would have been one year from the commencement of their service. While he viewed this request as justified, another volunteer unit was causing a disturbance by insisting that it be discharged so as to reach home by the end of the enlistment period; and in addition, this same unit supported their case by stating that because they were all exposed to malaria the previous year, the men should be allowed to depart before the season in question arrived. He assured the Secretary that he had taken measures to silence such talk and prevent its further spread. He then expressed the wish that the new regular regiments, which had recently been authorized by Congress, would arrive early.[44] On May 4th General Scott issued General Order #135, in which he reiterated the inclusion in an act of Congress the request that volunteers reconsider accepting their discharges and re-enlist for the duration of the war. He expressed his disappointment that there appeared to be little desire among the seven volunteer regiments to take such a step. And despite the delay it would create in prosecuting the war, he could not condemn those who had already proved their valor, nor direct them to engage the enemy just prior to being discharged, and then to undergo the risks of passing through a malaria infested Vera Cruz.[45]

Major General Winfield Scott

His earlier General Order #20, establishing martial law, did not stop the atrocities being committed by both volunteers and regulars. These acts, he stated, had remained unpunished because of lack of evidence to prove guilt. An exception was a volunteer who was tried by a military court of fellow volunteers. He was found guilty and received a jail sentence, plus a fine. To add to General Scott's problems, claims for redress of damages and grievances continued to mount; but the general, being without authority or means, could only curse the low behavior of those responsible.[46]

General Scott's preference for the regular soldier was further expressed by his words to the Secretary of War. He described the regulars setting up camp in a swift and efficient manner with never a movement wasted. Fifteen minutes was all they required to have everything done and supper on the fire. The volunteers, he claimed, often ate their supper cold, failed to erect their tents and subsequently slept exposed to the elements, were prone to neglect the care of their weapons with subsequent results often occurring in battle, and consequently, ran a greater risk of ending up in the hospital or an early grave.

Proceeding to the battlefield the general charged the volunteers with a lack of military precision, and a lack of confidence in each other. This confidence in the volunteers the general himself didn't have.[47] Immediately after occupying Mexico City General Scott appointed Maj. General Quitman as Military Governor. As he finished reading the orders firing was heard outside. Turning to an aide the general said—without determining the source of the disturbance:

> Will you have the kindness to go and say to our volunteer friends that it is unsoldier-like, bad manners, and dangerous to discharge arms in a city, and say to their officers that it must not occur again.[48]

Starting with President Polk's message to Congress of December 7, 1847, we gain a view into the distorted-for-political-reasons picture which was painted for public consumption. Placing ourselves back in time to that period, we hear that the army has gained everlasting glory on the battlefields of the war. Always outnumbered and assaulting strong defensive positions, the American soldiers, both the regular and volunteer troops have never faltered but always surged forward to victory. Just a few weeks after the last Congress adjourned, General Taylor, with less than five thousand men, practically all volunteers, gained a victory over General Santa Ana and his army of 20,000. Shortly thereafter Vera Cruz and its forts were seized in a brilliant action by General Scott.[49] W. L. Marcy, Secretary of War, echoed similar sentiments in his report to the President of December 2, 1847.[50] In a "Special Letter of Commendation" to Maj. General Taylor, the Secretary reiterated all the essential facts of the Victory at Buena Vista with patriotic wrappings, bestowing the highest praise on the nation's troops—and, consequently on the general.[51]

President James K. Polk

Moving a year closer to the present time we witness President James Polk on December 4, 1848, justify his call for volunteers in words which seem to bestow praise on himself as well. The late conflict, he claimed, proved once again that without any previous preparations for war, the volunteer soldiers were equal to any veteran troops, and could be called to their country's defense without any formal training being necessary. They could do so because of the familiarity gained in handling weapons from early youth—and many, particularly from the western states, were expert marksmen. Other factors which aided them in achieving their brilliant battle records were native intelligence, home reputations to maintain, and an individuality of character which was unique in the armies of mankind.[52]

Viewing that period from the present once again, we can see that the Americans of that time were the psychological and behavioral manifestation of individuality in its most extreme form:[53] fighting hard when there was fighting to be done, they couldn't be bothered with the idea of discipline, and the spit and polish of the regulars when the battles were over.[54] Their practice of selecting their own officers helped to enhance their sense of equality and left their spirit of individuality intact, but tended to be a negative factor to be overcome in striving for combat efficiency.[55] The element of fraud, or at least the suspicion of its existence, often entered these elections and furthered the possibility of failure in battle.[56] A prime example was the case of the company from Covington County, Mississippi. When the unit's 1st Lieutenant was elected the losers went home—all the way from Mexico. Subsequently, the home folks raised more funds and sent them back. General Scott, while allowing them to remain, left them on their own. They were then named the "Do As They Please Company."[57]

One Compton Smith served under General Taylor as "Acting Surgeon." He saw the initial volunteers as those motivated by the highest reasons. They were young in age, usually possessed a good education (for the time), felt the surge of patriotism and the necessity of taking home a good record. Among the southern volunteers the Mississippi Rifles and Texas Rangers were the most outstanding. Barely one-tenth of the original men of these two units lived to return home. Contrary to the image created, the first Texas Rangers were brave and respectable veterans of Texas's War of Independence. These men were distinctly different, and far above the sewer lice who came later in the interest of plunder.[58]

The picture which has evolved of the volunteer, that civilian soldier, is a portrait in paradox. And underlying this contradictory picture is the driving power and primary characteristic of the 19th century American—individualism! And furthermore, it effected, modified, influenced in one way or another, all other characteristics of these empire building adventurers. Manifest Destiny was the theme of the young American nation still suffering from growing pains, and these rough individualistic volunteers made its achievement a reality. However, despite what the volunteers had helped to create, it is, I believe, abundantly clear that unchecked and raw individualism is essentially a negative characteristic in the successful prosecution of a war. In battle it is an anti-cohesive element that can be triggered by the slightest unforeseen event—causing a bravely charging unit to turn into a cowardly mob fleeing in panic in the span of a few seconds. In camp it was manifested in the lack of systematic sanity requirements, organization, and control; every man instead doing what he wanted, when he wanted, and in a manner of his own choosing. Consequently, for the sake of his individuality, whether he elected to call it honor, equality, or simply being his own man, the volunteer in Mexico was seven times more likely to die from disease than from an enemy bullet. In town this same individualism was frequently expressed in an arrogant racism and violent display of ethnocentric behavior toward the Mexican civilians who were at their mercy. And the crudest and roughest elements of the volunteers were the ones, who in their own country, were most often in violation of their community's norms and taboos.[59]

Since the volunteer in the past had submitted only to his own dictates—within the framework of a loose conformity to society's requirements—he not only resented discipline imposed by others,[60] but tended to be oversensitive to even imagined threats to his sense of personal honor and self. Consequently, he would often perceive snubs, insults, etc., from meaningless and unintended remarks and gestures. He was often an impractical idealist who believed that equality could be practiced in all situations—only, however, among his own countrymen—and furthermore, damn well, should be! When he found that the army didn't share the same belief, when they tried to harness him with discipline and conformity, he rebelled—and frequently in the most violent manner.

 The only real difference between the regular soldier of the Mexican War and the civilian volunteer was that of training. However, that single difference was the major factor! Because, training brought control and organization, group action as one, helped to preserve health and life, created pride in self and respect for others—and—turned the wild individualism of the volunteers into the powerful controlled force of cohesive professional troops, who still retained the more positive aspects of American Individualism.[61]

Endnotes

Chapter 1
1. U.S. Congress, House, *Brig. General Taylor's Report of Apr. 26th*, H.E. Doc. #196, 29th Cong., 1st Sess. (1846), 120.
2. U.S. Congress, Senate, *President Polk's Message of December 7th*, S.E. Doc #1, 30th Cong., 1st Sess. (1847), 4.
3. *Taylor's Report of Apr. 26th*, H.E. Doc. #196, 29th Cong., 1st Sess. (1846), 120.
4. Jeremiah Hughes, ed., *Niles' National Register*, Vol. 70 (75 Vols.; Baltimore, 1846), 193; and from "Command of the Army," Ibid., July 4th, 276. Since General Taylor was only a brevet Brig. General, he was promoted to Maj. General in order to ensure his seniority among all the officers who might be assigned to the war zone.
5. U.S. Congress, Senate, *Secretary of War's Report of Dec. 5th*, S.E. Doc. #1, 29th Cong., 2nd Sess. (1846), 47.
6. U S. Congress, House, *Adjutant General's Report of Nov. 30th*, H.E. Doc. #8, 30th Cong., 1st Sess. (1847), 74–75.
7. Ibid., 78.
8. Hughes, "Response of the State Authorities," *Niles' National Register*, Vol. 70 (1846), 199.
9. Ibid., 162.
10. *Taylor's Report of Apr. 26th*, H.E. Doc. #196, 29th Cong., 1st Sess. (1846), 120.

11. Brig. General Cadmus M. Wilcox (prepared for the press by his niece: Mary Rachel Wilcox), *History of the Mexican War* (Washington, D.C.: The Church News Publishing Co., 1892), 76–78.
12. Hughes, "Maj. General Taylor's Report of May 20th to the Adjutant General of the Army," *Niles' National Register*, Vol. 70 (1846), 255.
13. Ibid., "Response of the State Authorities," 199–200.
14. Ibid., "Volunteers for the Army of Invasion," 202.
15. Ibid., "Disbanded Volunteers," 312.
16. Ibid., 371.
17. A Member of the Bloody First, *Reminiscences of a Campaign in Mexico* (Nashville: John York and Co., 1849), 60–61.
18. Ibid., 63–64.
19. Ibid., 68–69.
20. Wilcox, *History of the Mexican War*, 137–138.
21. Hughes, "Expedition Against Santa Fe," *Niles National Register*, Vol. 70 (1846), 400.
22. George Winston Smith and Charles Judah, eds., *Chronicles of the Gringos* (Albuquerque: University of New Mexico Press, 1968), 36–37, citing "Volunteers," Niles National Register, Vol. 70 (1846), 325–326.
23. Hughes, "A Heroine," *Niles' National Register* (1846), 288.
24. J. Jacob Oswandel, *Notes of the Mexican War 1846–47–48* (Philadelphia, 1885), 16–18.
25. Ibid., 22, 27.
26. Ibid., 33–34.
27. Ibid., 37–40.
28. Ibid., 42–43.
29. Captain Joseph Hill, First Pennsylvania Regiment, Ltr. To Brig. General Calwalader, *Calwalader Papers*, Baltimore, Maryland, February 26, 2847.
30. A Member of the Bloody First, *Reminiscences of a Campaign in Mexico*, 71–72.

31. Hughes, "Volunteers," *Niles National Register*, Vol. 70 (1846), 343.
32. Ibid., 311.
33. Oswandel, *Notes of the Mexican War*, 16–18.
34. Ibid., 44.
35. A Member of the Bloody First, *Reminiscences of a Campaign in Mexico*, 73–74.
36. Dr. S. Compton Smith, *Chile Con Carne; or the Camp and the Field* (New York: Miller and Curtis, 1857), 15–20.
37. Ibid., 28–29.
38. Hughes, "Loss of the Transport Ship *Ondiaka* with Troops on Board," *Niles' National Register*, Vol. 71 (1847), 401.
39. *Daily National Intelligencer* (Washington, D.C., October 19, 1846), 4.
40. U.S. Congress, Senate, *Secretary of War's Report of Dec. 2nd*, S.E. Doc. #1, 30th Cong., 1st Sess. (1847), 54.
41. Smith and Judah, *Chronicles of the Gringos*, 126–127, citing St. Jeremy F. Gilmer, Corps of Engineers, Santa Fe, to Captain George L. Weicher, Washington, D.C., November 6, 1846, Lenior Family Papers, Group II, So. Hist. Col. Nea.
42. *Daily National Intelligencer* (October 19, 1846), 4.
43. Hughes, "The Present Condition of the Army," *Niles' National Register*, Vol. 71 (1847), 279–280.

CHAPTER 2
1. Smith and Judah, *Chronicles of the Gringos*, 126–127, citing Lieutenant Gilmer, Lenior Family Papers.
2. *Secretary of War's Report of December 2nd*, S.E, Doc. #1, 30th Cong., 1st Sess. (1847), 55.
3. Smith and Judah, *Chronicles of the Gringos*, 125–127, citing Lieutenant Gilmer, Lenoir Family Papers.
4. Ibid., 133–134, citing "From Santa Fe and California!" *St. Louis Missouri Republican* (September 7, 1847).

5. Hughes, "Extract of a Letter dated Santa Fe, New Mexico, December 5, 1846," *Niles' National Register*, Vol. 72 (1847), 32.
6. *Daily National Intelligencer* (April 20, 1847), 4.
7. Hughes, "From a Letter dated Camp Belknap, Mexico, August 2, 1846," *Niles' National Register*, Vol. 71 (1847), 21.
8. John R. Kenly, *Memoirs of a Maryland Volunteer* (Philadelphia: J. B. Lippincott and Company, 1873), 45. The Baltimore Battalion was made up of three companies from Baltimore and two from the District of Columbia.
9. Hughes, "From a Letter dated Camp Belknap, Mexico, August 2, 1846," *Niles' National Register*, Vol. 71 (1847), 21.
10. Kenly, *Memoirs of a Maryland Volunteer*, 45, 47–48.
11. Smith and Judah, *Chronicles of the Gringos*, citing Colonel Henry R. Jackson, Camp Belknap near Burrita to Miss Martha J. Jackson, Monroe, Georgia, August 9, 1846, Jackson-Prine Papers, So. Hist. Col. Nea; and "From the Savannah Republican, Georgia, September 7, 1846," cited in *Niles' National Register*, Vol. 71 (1846), 88.
12. Smith, *Chile Con Carne; or the Camp and the Field*, 301–304.
13. A Member of the Bloody First, *Reminiscences of a Campaign in Mexico*, 93.
14. Oswandel, *Notes of the Mexican War 1846–47–48*; 173.
15. Ibid., 146.
16. Ibid., 390.
17. Ibid., 483–484.
18. Smith and Judah, *Chronicles of the Gringos*, 424–425, citing Colonel Robert Treat Paine, Regiment of North Carolina Volunteers.
19. *The Daily Picayune* (February 11, 1848).
20. Smith, *Chile Con Carne; or the Camp and the Field*, 66–68.
21. Oswandel, *Notes of the Mexican War 1846–47–48*; 82.
22. *Daily National Intelligencer* (January 1, 1847), citing the *New Orleans Delta* newspaper.

23. Hughes, "Affairs at Monterey," *Niles' National Register*, Vol. 71 (1846), 180, citing the *Charleston Mercury* newspaper.
24. U.S. Congress, House, *Maj. General Taylor's Report of May 23rd*, H.E. Doc. #56, 30th Cong., 1st Sess. (1847), 328.
25. Captain E. Kirby Smith (prepared for the press by his daughter: Emma Jerome Blackwood), *To Mexico with Scott* (Cambridge: Harvard University Press, 1919), 63.
26. Oswandel, *Notes of the Mexican War 1846–47–48*; 154–155, 158.
27. U.S. Congress, House, *Maj. General Taylor's Report of June 16th*, H.E. #56, 30th Cong., 1st Sess. (1847), 368.
28. *The American Star* (November 3, 1847). Published in Mexico by the authority of the Hdqtrs. of the Army.
29. *Maj. General Taylor's Report of June 16th*, H.E. #56, 30th Cong., 1st Sess. (1847), 368.
30. *The American Star* (November 3, 1847).
31. *Maj. General Taylor's Report of June 16th*, H.E. #56, 30th Cong., 1st Sess. (1847), 368.
32. *Statement of Nicholas Dorich*, Ibid., 128.
33. Pedro Vander Linden, M.D., "Report of a Mexican Doctor," *The New Orleans Medical and Surgical Journal*, IV (April 19, 1847), 267–268. Dr. Linden was the Surgeon General of the Mexican Army.
34. A Member of the Bloody First, *Reminiscences of a Campaign in Mexico*, 252–253.
35. Oswandel, *Notes of the Mexican War 1846–47–48*; 390–392.
36. *The Daily Picayune* (February 11, 1848).
37. *The Daily National Intelligencer* (January 1, 1847), 4.
38. Smith and Judah, *Chronicles of the Gringos*, 431–434, citing Francis B. Heitman, *Historical Register and Dictionary of the United States Army*, II (Washington: Gov't Prtg. Office, 1903), 282.
39. Hughes, "The Irish Legion," *Niles' National Register*, Vol. 72; 22.

40. Smith and Judah, *Chronicles of the Gringos*, 431–434, citing Francis B. Heitman, *Historical Register and Dictionary of the United States Army.*
41. *The American Star* (September 20, 1847).
42. *The Daily Picayune* (June 15, 1848).
43. Ibid., (April 13, 1848).
44. Hughes, "Deserters from the Army," *Niles' National Register,* Vol. 72 (1847), 32.

CHAPTER 3
1. Wilcox, *History of the Mexican War,* 561.
2. Smith and Judah, *Chronicles of the Gringos,* 30, citing Maj. General Scott, "The Brassos," to William L. Marcy, January 16, 1847, William L. Marcy, DLC.
3. Hughes, "Volunteers: Illinois Volunteers in the West," *Niles' National Register,* Vol. 71 (1846), 118.
4. Ibid., "Santa Fe" (January 9, 1847), 290.
5. Ibid., Vol. 72 (1846), 7–8.
6. Ibid., 8.
7. *Daily National Intelligencer* (March 9, 1847).
8. A Member of the Bloody First, *Reminiscences of a Campaign in Mexico,* 81.
9. Ibid., 87–89.
10. Ibid., 108–109.
11. Smith, *Chile Con Carne; or the Camp and the Field,* 65.
12. *Daily National Intelligencer* (October 16, 1846).
13. A Member of the Bloody First, *Reminiscences of a Campaign in Mexico,* 110–111.
14. D. E. Livingston, ed., *The Mexican War Diary of Thomas D. Tennery* (Norman: University of Oklahoma Press, 1970), 16–18, 22, 25. Tennery was a private in the 4th Regiment of Illinois Volunteers 1846–1847.
15. Ibid., 32.
16. Ibid., 25–26.

17. Ibid., 26.
18. Ibid., 28.
19. Hughes, *Niles' National Register*, Vol. 71 (1846), 122.
20. Livingston, *The Mexican Mar Diary of Thomas D. Tennery*, 36.
21. Ibid., 37.
22. Ibid., 45.
23. Hughes, "A Letter from a Correspondent of the Nashville Blues," *Niles' National Register*, Vol. 71 (1846), 119. Lieutenant E. Eastman wrote the letter on September 11, 1846, from a camp near Camargo.
24. *Daily National Intelligencer* (October 26, 1846), 3, citing the *Milledgeville Recorder* of October 20, 1846, Milledgeville, Georgia.
25. Ibid., citing the *Charleston Evening News*, Charleston, South Carolina.
26. Ibid., (October 20, 1846), 3, citing the *Kentucky Observer* of October 14th, cited from a letter by James S. Jackson.
27. Hughes, "Army Journal," *Niles' National Register*, Vol. 71 (1846), 122, citing the *Kentucky Observer* of October 14th, cited from a letter by James S. Jackson.
28. Ibid., 120.
29. Ibid., "Signed D" (November 21, 1846), 266.
30. Wilcox, *History of the Mexican War*, 199.
31. Oswandel, *Notes of the Mexican War 1846–47–48*; 142–144.
32. Ibid., 146.
33. Ibid., 148.
34. Ibid., 155.
35. "Ltr. from Dr. C. Rieul to Brig. General Calwalader," *Calwalader Papers* (May 4, 1847).
36. "Ltr. from Dr. Albert C. Renasey to Brig. General Calwalader," *Calwalader Papers* (May 4, 1847).
37. Thomas N. Love, M.D., "Remarks on Some of the Diseases Which Prevailed in the Second Regiment Mississippi Rifles,

for the First Six Months of its Service," *The New Orleans Medical and Surgical Journal*, V (1848), 1.
38. Ibid., 4–5.
39. Ibid., 140.
40. Ibid.
41. Tudor McCormick, M.D., "Ltr. to Dr. Love," *New Orleans Medical and Surgical Journal*, IV (June 22, 1847), 140. Dr. McCormick held the post of Medical Purveyor of the U.S. Army.
42. Oswandel, *Notes of the Mexican War*, 195–196.
43. Ibid., 215.
44. Ibid., 223.
45. Ibid., 267.
46. Ibid., 286.
47. Ibid., 435.
48. Wilcox, *History of the Mexican War*, 337.
49. Ibid., 554.
50. Ibid., 561.

CHAPTER 4
1. Hughes, "Secretary of War's Report of December 5, 1846," *Niles' National Register*, Vol. 71 (1847), 149.
2. Wilcox, *History of the Mexican War*, 138.
3. Hughes, "Santa Fe," *Niles' National Register*, Vol. 70 (1845), 95.
4. Ibid., "From the Diary of an Officer of the Army of the West," Vol. 71 (1847), 92.
5. Ibid., "Secretary of War's Report of December 5, 1846," 149.
6. Ibid., "From the Diary of an Officer of the Army of the West," 92.
7. *Daily National Intelligencer* (November 1, 1846).
8. Hughes, "Correspondent of the St. Louis Republican, October 20th," *Niles' National Register*, Vol. 71 (1847), 226.
9. *Daily National Intelligencer* (November 1, 1846).

10. Wilcox, *History of the Mexican War*, 153.
11. Ibid., 155–158.
12. Hughes, "Illinois Volunteers in the West, August 24, 1846," *Niles' National Register*, Vol. 71 (1847), 118.
13. Ibid., "Letter from Captain Geo. T. M. David, Aid–de–Camp to Brig. General Shields," 262.
14. Ibid., "Secretary of War's Report of December 5, 1846," 249.
15. Ibid., "Letter from Captain Chapman to General Worth, January 25, 1847," 401; and *Maj. General Taylor's Report of January 30th* and *Brig. General Wool's Report of January 27th*, H.E. #56, 30th Cong., 1st. Sess. (1847), 296–298.
16. George Wilkins Kendall, *The War Between the United States and Mexico* (Philadelphia: George S. Appleton Co., 1851), 2.
17. Smith, *To Mexico with Scott*, 63.
18. Hughes, "Volunteer Division at Monterey," *Niles' National Register*, Vol. 71 (1846), 102.
19. *Daily National Intelligencer* (October 12, 1846), 3, citing the *Daily Picayune*, New Orleans.
20. A Member of the Bloody First, *Reminiscences of a Campaign in Mexico*, 136–141.
21. Hughes, "The Tennessee Volunteers," *Niles' National Register*, Vol. 71 (1847), 160.
22. A Member of the Bloody First, *Reminiscences of a Campaign in Mexico*, 146.
23. Hughes, "The Tennessee Volunteers." *Niles' National Register*, Vol. 71 (1847), 160.
24. Ibid., "The Baltimore Battalion in the Battle of Monterey," 156, citing the *Baltimore American*.
25. Kenly, *Memoirs of a Maryland Volunteer*, 107–108.
26. Hughes, "The Baltimore Battalion in the Battle of Monterey," *Niles' National Register*, Vol. 71 (1847), 156.
27. Kenly, *Memoirs of a Maryland Volunteer*, 107–108.
28. Ibid., 112.

29. Hughes, "The Baltimore Battalion in the Battle of Monterey," *Niles' National Register*, Vol. 71 (1840), 156.
30. Ibid., "Siege of Monterey," 154.
31. Ibid., "The Baltimore Battalion in the Battle of Monterey," 156.
32. Kenly, *Memoirs of a Maryland Volunteer*, 112–114.
33. Hughes, "Report of Brig. General Quitman," *Niles' National Register*, Vol. 71 (1847), 220.
34. A Member of the Bloody First, *Reminiscences of a Campaign in Mexico*, 147.
35. Hughes, "Report of Brig. General Quitman," *Niles' National Register*, Vol. 71 (1847), 220.
36. A Member of the Bloody First, *Reminiscences of a Campaign in Mexico*, 148.
37. Wilcox, *History of the Mexican War*, 104.
38. Hughes, "Report of Brig. General Quitman," *Niles' National Register*, Vol. 71 (1847), 220.
39. Kendall, *The War Between the United States and Mexico*, 8.
40. Hughes, "Report of Brig. General Quitman," *Niles' National Register*, Vol. 71 (1847), 220.
41. Ibid., "The Tall Yankee Clerk," 155, citing the *New Orleans Picayune*.
42. *Daily National Intelligencer* (October 12, 1846).
43. Smith, *To Mexico with Scott*, 63.
44. Ibid., (November 2, 1846), citing the *New Orleans Picayune*'s Special Correspondent, Monterey, September 27, 1846.
45. Kenly, *Memoirs of Maryland Volunteer*, 174.
46. Ibid., 180.
47. Ibid., 191.
48. Kendall, *The War Between the United States and Mexico*, 11.
49. *Secretary of War's Report of December 2*, S.E. Doc. #1, 30th Cong., 1st Sess. (1847), 48.
50. Kenly, *Memoirs of a Maryland Volunteer*, 259–262.

51. J. Frost, *The Mexican War and Its Warriors* (New Haven and Philadelphia: H. Mansfield, 1848), 109–110.
52. U.S. Congress, Senate, *Maj. General Taylor's Report of March 6*, S.E. Doc. #1, 30th Cong., 1st Sess. (1847), 132.
53. Ibid., 137–148.
54. *Daily National Recorder* (April 21, 1847).
55. Kendall, *The War Between the United States and Mexico*, 12.
56. Ibid.
57. Ibid., 12–13.
58. Wilcox, *History of the Mexican War*, 224.
59. *Taylor's Report of March 6*, S.E. Doc. #1, 30th Cong., 1st Sess. (1847), 133–134.
60. Kendall, *The War Between the United States and Mexico*, 13.
61. Ibid., 14.
62. Ibid., 15.
63. Ibid., 15–16.
64. *Taylor's Report of March 6*, S.E. Doc. #1, 30th Cong., 1st Sess. (1847), 142.
65. Smith, *Chile Con Carne; or the Camp and the Field*, 250.
66. *Secretary of War's Report of December 2nd*, S.E. Doc. #1, 30th Cong., 1st Sess. (1847), 47.
67. Ibid., 49.
68. Kendall, *The War Between the United States and Mexico*, 18.
69. U.S. Congress, Senate, *Maj. General Scott's Report of April 23rd*, S.E. Doc. #1, 30th Cong., 1st Sess. (1847), 261–262.
70. See bottom center of the "Battle of Cerro Gordo" Map, page 75.
71. Kendall, *The War Between the United States and Mexico*, 24.
72. A Member of the Bloody First, *Reminiscences of a Campaign in Mexico*, 248.
73. Kendall, *The War Between the United States and Mexico*, 25.
74. A Member of the Bloody First, *Reminiscences of a Campaign in Mexico*, 249.
75. Kendall, *The War Between the United States and Mexico*, 25.

76. A Member of the Bloody First, *Reminiscences of a Campaign in Mexico*, 249.
77. Kendall, *The War Between the United States and Mexico*, 27.
78. Lieut. General Winfield Scott, *Memoirs of Lieut. General Scott, LLD.*, Vol. II (2 Vols.; New York: Sheldon and Company, 1864), 477–479.
79. Kendall, *The War Between the United States and Mexico*, 30–32.
80. Ibid., 43.
81. Wilcox, *History of the Mexican War*, 483.
82. Ibid., 561.
83. *The Daily Picayune* (June 15, 1848).

CHAPTER 5
1. Hughes, "Recruiting for the Army," *Niles' National Register*, Vol. 70 (1846), 293.
2. Ibid., "A Ltr. from Matamoros, August 11, 1846," Vol. 71 (1846), 58.
3. *Daily National Intelligencer* (October 20, 1846), citing the *New Orleans Bee* of October 12th.
4. Ibid., November 2nd, citing Colonel Balie Peyton, September 25, 1846.
5. Hughes, "Ltr. from Captain K. Bronaugh, Co. E., Baltimore Battalion, September 27, 1846," *Niles' National Register*, Vol. 71, 157.
6. Ibid., "Report of General Quitman," Vol. 71 (1847), 220–221.
7. *Daily National Intelligencer* (October 12, 1846).
8. Hughes, "Report of General Quitman," *Niles' National Register*, Vol. 71 (1847), 221.
9. *Daily National Intelligencer* (January 19, 1847), citing a Ltr. from Major Giddings.
10. Hughes, "Report of General Quitman," *Niles' National Register*, Vol. 71 (1847), 221.

11. Ibid., "Monterey, November 11, 1846," 265.
12. Wilcox, *History of the Mexican War*, 237–238.
13. *Daily National Intelligencer* (April 19, 1847).
14. Ibid., citing the *Daily Picayune*.
15. Hughes, *Niles' National Register*, Vol. 72 (1847), 83.
16. Frost, *The Mexican War and Its Warriors*, 119–120.
17. Smith, *To Mexico with Scott*, 63–65.
18. Ibid., 83–84.
19. Ibid., 89.
20. Ibid., 47.
21. Ibid., 7.
22. Since Captain Smith was in several battles in which the San Patricio Battalion also participated, he could hardly have been unaware of its existence; or, of the desertions from the regular army which was the source of its manpower.
23. Smith, *To Mexico with Scott*, 151–152.
24. Smith and Judah, *Chronicles of the Gringos*, 39–40, citing Lieutenant Thomas Williams, Hdqtrs. of the Army, Ship Mass. off Gobor Island, to John R. Williams, Detroit, February 28, 1847.
25. Ibid., 24.
26. U.S. Congress, Senate, *Brig. General Lane's Report of February 25th*, S.E. Doc. #1, 30th Cong., 1st Sess. (1847), 183–184.
27. Ibid., *Colonel Jefferson Davis' Report of March 2nd*, 191–192.
28. Ibid., *Captain T. W. Sherman's Report of March 2nd*, 204.
29. Smith and Judah, *Chronicles of the Gringos*, 27, citing Colonel William B. Campbell, Camp near Jalupa, to David Campbell, April 25, 1847, David Campbell Papers, Duke.
30. *Daily National Intelligencer* (October 31, 1846), 3, citing the *New Orleans Tropic* of October 21, 1846.
31. Hughes, *Niles' National Register*, Vol. 70 (1846), 403.
32. *Letters of Zachary Taylor from the Battlefields of the Mexican War* (Rochester, New York, 1908), 51, citing the originals

in the Collection of Mr. William K. Bixby of St. Louis, Missouri.
33. Ibid., 75.
34. Ibid., 119.
35. *Daily National Intelligencer* (October 14, 1846), 3.
36. Hughes, *Niles' National Register*, Vol. 71 (1847), 165.
37. Smith, *Chile Con Carne; or the Camp and the Field*, 299–301.
38. Ibid., 303–304.
39. *Taylor's Report of March 6th*, S.E. Doc. #1, 30th Cong., 1st Sess. (1847), 138–140.
40. *Taylor's Report of May 23rd*, H.E. Doc. #56, 30th Cong., 1st Sess. (1847), 138–140.
41. U.S. Congress, Senate, *Maj. General Patterson's Report of March 14th*, S.E. Doc. #1, 30th Cong., 1st Sess. (1847), 247–248.
42. Hughes, *Niles' National Register*, Vol. 70 (1846), 214–215, citing the *Philadelphia North American* of 24 May, 1846.
43. U.S. Congress, House, *Maj. General Scott's Report of April 5th*, H.E. Doc. #56, 30th Cong., 1st Sess. (1847), 100.
44. Ibid.
45. Ibid., *Maj. General Scott's Report of May 6th*, 144.
46. Ibid., *Maj. General Scott's General Order #87*, 104.
47. Smith and Judah, *Chronicles of the Gringos*, 30, citing Maj. General Scott, "The Brassos, to William L. Marcy, January 16, 1847, William L. Marcy Papers, DLC.
48. Wilcox, *History of the Mexican War*, 484.
49. U.S. Congress, Senate, *President Polk's Message of December 7th*, S.E. Doc. #1, 30th Cong., 1st Sess. (1847), 5.
50. Ibid., *Secretary of War's Report of December 2nd*, 48–49.
51. U.S. Congress, House, *Secretary of War's Letter to General Taylor*, H.E. Doc. #56, 30th Cong., 1st Sess. (1847), 308.
52. U.S. Congress, Senate, *President Polk's Message of December 5th*, 30th Cong., 2nd Sess. (1848), 9.
53. Conclusions of the author of this thesis.

54. Smith and Judah, *Chronicles of the Gringos*, 36, citing "James Crabb to Henry H. Keeling," July 14, 1846, Western American MSS, Beinecke.
55. Conclusions of the author of this thesis.
56. Smith and Judah, *Chronicles of the Gringos*, 37–38, citing "Volunteers," *Niles' National Register*, Vol. 70 (1846), 325–326, and Jeel R. Poinsett, "The Homestead," to Gouverneur Kemble, Cold Spring, New York, July 27, 1846, Gilpin-Poinsett Papers, Hist. Sec. Pa.
57. Ibid., 38, citing "Kenneth McKennzie, Covington County, Mississippi, to Duncan McLauring, Richmond County, North Carolina, n.d. fragment of a letter," Duncan-McLaurin Papers, Duke.
58. Ibid., 42–43, citing S. Compton Smith, *Chile Con Carne; or the Camp and the Field*, 292–295.
59. Conclusions of the author.
60. Smith and Judah, *Chronicles of the Gringos*, 424, citing Colonel Robert Treat Paine, Regiment of North Carolina Volunteers.
61. Conclusions of the author.

Bibliography

A Member of the Bloody First. *Reminiscences of a Campaign in Mexico*. Nashville: John York and Co., 1849.
American Star. Mexico.
Calwalader, Brig. General George. *The Calwalader Papers*.
Daily National Intelligencer. Washington, D.C.
Daily Picayune. New Orleans.
Frost, J. *The Mexican War and Its Warriors*. New Haven and Philadelphia: H. Mansfield, 1848.
Hill, Captain Joseph. *Ltr. to Brig. General Calwalader*. Calwalader Papers. Baltimore, Maryland, February 26, 1847.
Hughes, Jeremiah, ed., *Niles' National Register*. 75 Vols. Baltimore, 1811–1849.
Kendall, George Wilkins. *The War Between the United States and Mexico*. Philadelphia: George S. Appleton Co., 1851.
Kenly, John R. *Memoirs of a Maryland Volunteer*. Philadelphia: J. B. Lippincott and Co., 1873.
Livingston, D. E. ed. *The Mexican War Diary of Thomas D. Tennery*. Norman: University of Oklahoma Press, 1970.
New Orleans Medical and Surgical Journal. New Orleans.
Oswandel, J. Jacob. *Notes of the Mexican War 1846–47–48*. Cambridge: Harvard University Press, 1917.
Scott, Lieut. General Winfield. *Memoirs of Lieut. General Scott LLD*. New York: Sheldon and Company, 1864.

Smith, George Winston, and Judah, Charles. *Chronicles of the Gringos.*

Smith, Captain E. Kirby. *To Mexico with Scott.* Cambridge: Harvard University Press, 1917.

Smith, S. Compton. *Chile Con Carne; or the Camp and the Field.* New York: Miller and Curtis, 1857.

Taylor, Maj; General Zachary. *Letters of Zachary Taylor From the Battlefields of the Mexican War.* St. Louis: Collection of Mr. William K. Bixby.

U.S. Congress. House. H.E. Doc. #196, 29th Cong., 1st Sess., 1846.

U.S. Congress. House. H.D. Doc. #8, 30th Cong., 1st Sess., 1847.

U.S. Congress. House. H.S. Doc. #56, 30th Cong., 1st Sess., 1847.

U.S. Congress. Senate. S.E. Doc. #1, 30th Cong., 2nd Sess., 1846.

U.S. Congress. Senate. S.E. Doc. #1, 30th Cong., 1st Sess., 1847.

Wilcox, Brig. General Cadmus H. *History of the Mexican War.* Washington, D.C.: The Church News Publishing Company, 1892.